Psalm 98:1

All *of* Your Wonderful Deeds

Psalms of Praise

CONCORDIA PUBLISHING HOUSE • SAINT LOUIS

Copyright © 2008 Concordia Publishing House
3558 S. Jefferson Ave.
St. Louis, MO 63118-3968

1-800-325-3040 • www.cph.org

By Jane Fryar, Christina Hergenrader, Lisa Hahn, Lisa Hellyer, Judy Henke, Jill Hasstedt, and Eva Rickman

Edited by Peggy Kuethe

Cover and interior illustrations © shutterstock.com

Unless otherwise indicated, Scripture quotations are from The Holy Bible, English Standard Version®. Copyright © 2001 by Crossway Bibles, a publishing ministry of Good News Publishers, Wheaton, Illinois. Used by permission. All rights reserved.

Hymn texts with the abbreviation *LSB* are from *Lutheran Service Book*, copyright © 2006 Concordia Publishing House. All rights reserved.

Quotation from *Reading the Psalms with Luther* is copyright © 2007 Concordia Publishing House.

This publication may be available in braille, in large print, or on cassette tape for the visually impaired. Please allow 8 to 12 weeks for delivery. Write to Lutheran Blind Mission, 7550 Watson Rd., St. Louis, MO 63119-4409; call toll free 1-888-215-2455; or visit the Web site: www.blindmission.org.

1 2 3 4 5 6 7 8 9 10   17 16 15 14 13 12 11 10 09 08

a new song

All *of* Your Wonderful Deeds
Psalms of Praise

Meet the Authors

Jane L. Fryar enjoys serving God's people by writing and teaching. Her books include two titles focused on servant leadership, several LifeLight courses, the popular *Today's Light* devotional materials, and various other curricula and resources for Christian teachers. Jane spends her spare time baking bread, lifting weights, and playing with Marty the Wonder Dog.

Christina Hergenrader is the wife of a supportive husband and mother to three amazing children. She writes contemporary Christian novels and is a university writing instructor. Christina writes the weekly W5 Online for Concordia Publishing House and is a frequent contributor to other CPH publications. "Sharing God's grace through fiction is a wonderful balance to motherhood. I can give my characters all the things I hope I'm teaching my children—love, joy, and the assurance they are forgiven children of God."

Lisa Hahn says that her favorite vocations in their North Wisconsin home are being wife to Kevin and mom to Noah, Anna, Nathanael, and Luke. Her family enjoys singing, their backyard, making up games, and answering the question frequently asked regarding their two terrier mutts: "So . . . what kind of dogs are those anyway?" Lisa enjoys homeschooling, baking, gardening, and God's daily reminders of our total dependence on Him in Christ.

Lisa Hellyer loves life and lives it to the full. She is "Aunt Lisa" to nine beautiful nieces and nephews and treasures her time with them. For more than twenty years, she has served the Church as a director of Christian education and is currently serving at Lord of Life in Leawood, Kansas. During football season, Lisa can be heard cheering loudly for the Miami Dolphins!

Judy Henke worked at Concordia Publishing House in marketing for eleven years before she was called by God to do mission work in Thailand. There she worked as a teacher of English as a second language and as a consultant for the LCMS in Southeast Asia for three years. Currently, Judy is the director of the International Friendship Center, an outreach ministry to international students at the University of Wisconsin.

Jill Hasstedt is wife to Frederick and mom to two sons, Aden and Kenan. Her "boys" keep her humble with merciless teasing and she is grateful for the only other female presence in their household, their cat, Paws. A second grade teacher, Jill also serves as director of family ministry at Zion Lutheran Church in Belleville, Illinois.

Eva Noel Rickman is a deaconess currently living in Iowa with her pastor-husband, Arthur, and their newborn daughter, Bethany Noel. They recently returned from the two years of service in the mission field in Latin America. Eva served in the areas of diaconal training and human care. Besides writing, she enjoys jogging, reading, quilting, and spending time with her family.

"I will give thanks
to the LORD with
my whole heart;
I will recount all of
Your wonderful deeds."

Psalm 9:1

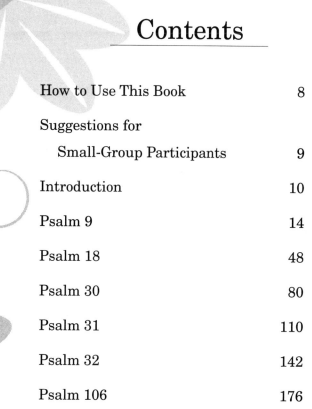

Contents

How to Use This Book

A New Song: All of Your Wonderful Deeds is designed to help you grow in faith in your Savior, Jesus Christ, and to see how God works in your life as His precious and redeemed daughter. It is not meant to consume large blocks of your time. Rather, this book will help you to weave God's Word into your day. It will also encourage and uplift you in your personal and small-group study of His Word.

A New Song: All of Your Wonderful Deeds provides you and your group with six weeks of faith narratives based on biblical psalms. Each faith narrative was written by a real woman facing real-life issues—just like you. Each of our authors found help, encouragement, and direction for her life from God's Word and now shares her true story with you in her own words. Following each faith narrative, you will find questions that will encourage your own personal reflection and help bring forth meaningful and fruitful conversation in the comfort and security of your small group.

To derive the greatest benefit from your study, read the psalm in its entirety at the beginning of the week, and review it from time to time. Allow the authors' reflections on God's work in their lives to inspire your own. Write your responses and thoughts in the margins, if you wish. Space is provided on the side of each page under the ✒ symbol. Answer the daily questions as best fits your unique situation and the time available to you, but consider how your responses can further group discussion. The prayers offered at the end of each narrative will help you to focus on the weekly theme and emphasis as you respond to God for His gifts of grace. Use the prayers as they are written, or make them your own, changing and adding to them as they touch your heart.

Our prayer is that this book will enrich you as you recount God's wonderful deeds—especially in sending His Son and our Savior, Jesus Christ—as you study His Holy Word.

—The Editor

Suggestions for Small-Group Participants

1. Before you begin, spend some time in prayer, asking God to strengthen your faith through the study of His Word. The Scriptures were written so that we might believe in Jesus Christ and have life in His name (John 20:31).

2. Take some time before the meeting to look over the session, review the psalm, and answer the questions.

3. As a courtesy to others, arrive on time.

4. Be an active participant. The leader will guide the group's discussion, not give a lecture.

5. Avoid dominating the conversation by answering every question or by giving unnecessarily long answers. On the other hand, avoid the temptation to not share at all.

6. Treat anything shared in your group as confidential until you have asked for and received permission to share it outside of the group. Treat information about others outside of your group as confidential until you have asked for and received permission to share it with group members.

7. Some participants may be new to Bible study or new to the Christian faith. Help them feel welcomed and comfortable.

8. Affirm other participants when you can. If someone offers what you perceive to be a "wrong" answer, ask the Holy Spirit to guide her to seek the correct answer from God's Word.

9. Keep in mind that the questions are discussion starters. Don't be afraid to ask additional questions that relate to the topic. Don't get the group off track.

10. If you are comfortable doing so, volunteer now and then to pray at the beginning or end of the session.

Jane L. Fryar

Introduction

"There are eight million stories in the naked city; this has been one of them." With these words, narrator Lawrence Dobkin closed each episode of the crime drama series *The Naked City* during its initial run from 1958 to 1959 and when it returned to air from 1960 to 1963. At first blush, we might be tempted to dismiss the series as one of the first to break into television's "shoot 'em up, cops and crooks" genre. But far from formulaic, *The Naked City* drew acclaim from critics for its psychological depth and complex characters. The scripts ended unpredictably, and viewers were often left wondering which characters fell in the hero column and which in the villain.

I admit it. I had to research the details in the paragraph above. In 1958, I was too young to take much interest in psychological exploration. *Howdy Doody* was more my cup of tea. (Or should I say, my cup of Ovaltine?) Nonetheless, I do remember the tag line: "There are eight million stories. . . ." Even back then, I aspired to write. And I wanted to tell some of those stories!

Behind Every Psalm . . .

Stories often convey what academic treatises with their detailed explanations cannot. This book, like the three others in the A New Song series, illustrates that. The psalms it explores invite us to tie the stories of our everyday lives to the stories of the faithful who have preceded us through the centuries. What's more, these psalms give us the words—words inspired by the Holy Spirit Himself—to help us do that.

Behind every psalm lies a story. We know some of those stories. The historical books of the Old Testament, combined with a bit of detective work on the part of Bible scholars, have helped us discern the context from which some of the psalms sprang. For instance, most reliable scholars believe King David wrote Psalm 51 as a prayer of repentance after his adulterous affair with Bathsheba. We have good reason to think that David also wrote Psalm 34, penning this hymn of praise after a narrow escape from the five lords of the Philistines before he became Israel's king. (He pretended to be insane, and the Philistines believed his act—a better than Oscar-winning performance! Compare Psalm 34 and 1 Samuel 21:10–15.)

Even so, the stories behind most of the psalms, including those you will read during this six-week study, lie shrouded in the mists of history. That does not, however, limit their power to touch and transform our hearts today. Even those who do not know the Good Shepherd sometimes turn in times of trouble and turmoil to the familiar cadences and comforting assurances that begin, "The LORD is my shepherd; I shall not want" (Psalm 23:1).

God's Story, Your Story, Our Story

The psalmists knew their own stories of turmoil, of danger, of fear, of thirst, and of neediness. They felt the oppressive weight of guilt as their consciences told and retold the stories of their yet unconfessed sins. Their hearts danced in the exhilaration of worship as they recalled the never-ending story of God's love and deliverance, of His promises and pardon. We need not know the details of their stories because their words express so powerfully the longing and the joys of our own hearts.

The authors of the faith narratives in this study guide provide a model to help readers make this connection. The honesty and the authenticity with which they write further deepens the truth that we are not alone in our struggles or in our joys. Surely, God is with us, just as the psalmists have said (e.g., Psalm 46:1). In addition, we can take comfort in knowing that our sisters in the faith understand and share in the adventure of love and trust to which our Lord calls us as we live out our various vocations as His redeemed daughters in a fallen world.

Despite the frustrations and fears, the dangers and temptations we meet along the way, we take courage from what someone has called the "blazing hope" that flows to us from our Savior's cross and open tomb. Connected to Him in our Baptism and nourished for our journey in the Holy Supper, we trust that our stories will honor our Lord here on earth and will continue to do that in the eternal glories of the home we have inherited from Him.

Celebrate His Wonderful Deeds

The hope our Savior gives is not some pious wish or improbable dream. It is as sure as His open, empty grave and as certain as His return to judge the living and the dead. And because it is so, our lives tell the story of thankfulness, the story of praise for His goodness, the story of service and of witness to His love.

Each psalm included in this book helps us in its own way express the joy in our hearts for all the wonderful deeds our God has done. Together, these psalms help us celebrate the miracles of creation, of deliverance from evil, of forgiveness, and of sanctification. They help us consider the many ways the story of our Savior's love has intersected with our own life stories, weaving a tapestry of grace that will evoke our awe and thankfulness throughout all eternity.

One day, many more than eight million stories of God's grace for us in Jesus Christ will be told in the heavenly city. May your story be one of them, and may it bring your Lord glory and you yourself endless joy!

Week One

Psalm 9

¹ I will give thanks to the LORD with my whole heart;
I will recount all of Your wonderful deeds.

² I will be glad and exult in You;
I will sing praise to Your name, O Most High.

³ When my enemies turn back,
they stumble and perish before Your presence.

⁴ For You have maintained my just cause;
You have sat on the throne, giving righteous judgment.

⁵ You have rebuked the nations; You have made the wicked perish;
You have blotted out their name forever and ever.

⁶ The enemy came to an end in everlasting ruins;
their cities You rooted out;
the very memory of them has perished.

⁷ But the LORD sits enthroned forever;
He has established His throne for justice,

⁸ and He judges the world with righteousness;
He judges the peoples with uprightness.

⁹ The LORD is a stronghold for the oppressed,
a stronghold in times of trouble.

¹⁰ And those who know Your name put their trust in You,
for You, O LORD, have not forsaken those who seek You.

¹¹ Sing praises to the LORD, who sits enthroned in Zion!
Tell among the peoples His deeds!

¹² For He who avenges blood is mindful of them;
He does not forget the cry of the afflicted.

¹³ Be gracious to me, O LORD!
See my affliction from those who hate me,
O You who lift me up from the gates of death,

¹⁴ that I may recount all Your praises,
that in the gates of the daughter of Zion
I may rejoice in Your salvation.

¹⁵ The nations have sunk in the pit that they made;
in the net that they hid, their own foot has been caught.

¹⁶ The LORD has made Himself known; He has executed judgment;
the wicked are snared in the work of their own hands.
Higgaion. Selah

¹⁷ The wicked shall return to Sheol,
all the nations that forget God.

¹⁸ For the needy shall not always be forgotten,
and the hope of the poor shall not perish forever.

¹⁹ Arise, O LORD! Let not man prevail;
let the nations be judged before You!

²⁰ Put them in fear, O LORD!
Let the nations know that they are but men! *Selah*

Christina Hergenrader

Psalm 9:1–4

I will give thanks to the LORD with my whole heart; I will recount all of Your wonderful deeds. I will be glad and exult in You; I will sing praise to Your name, O Most High.

His Wonderful Deeds, Indeed!

When my husband turned twenty-five, he started running marathons, and I became a marathon spectator. I guess that sounds lazy—if it's noble to finish a marathon, then watching from the sidelines is the hobby of underachievers.

But at Mike's first marathon, I quickly learned that cheering for your favorite runner is challenging too. Okay, not as challenging as running 26 miles, but there's still an awful lot of running around, map reading, defensive driving, and mathematical equations—as well as screaming and jumping up and down—that go into being a fan.

Mike has always dreamed of qualifying for the Boston Marathon. To do that, he would have to run 26 miles in just a little over three hours—roughly seven minutes a mile. Mike trained for months before his first preparatory marathon. In the weeks before race day, he did everything to prepare himself for this event. He limited his diet to simple carbs and lean protein. He saw the sun rise while running around the track and saw it set from the track too. He was determined to master a seven-minute pace in order to meet his goal.

I was so excited for him as he ran, literally, after his dream. I approached my job as cheerleader, too, with the same careful planning. I received tips from others whose loved ones had run the local marathon. For example, I bought Mike a bright yellow shirt so I could pick him out of the crowd. I also put together a race map to navigate the roads around the marathon course, which are full of closures and detours. I wanted to park as close as possible to the course so I could jump out and cheer for Mike as he ran by. It took all my left-brain power to determine the right places to park and (according to a mathematical equation my engineer-trained husband worked out for me) what time I needed to be at each spot. Of course, every minute made a difference. If he ran slower or faster than planned, he would arrive at a location a minute or two sooner or later than I. And if I lost track of his pace, I might not see him for the rest of the race.

By race day, both of us were ready. He pushed his way into the crush of nervous runners. I hopped into our car, armed with my map, calculator, and cell phone so I could call friends who were tracking Mike's progress on the Internet.

However, with all my careful planning, I still wasn't prepared for my first stop. I arrived a few minutes early, and when

Christina

17

I saw Mike's distinctive gait (and even more distinctive yellow shirt) as he ran, a passionate, excited look on his face, I lost it. He was early! He was doing great—ahead of his goal pace.

"You're doing it!" I screamed. "You're doing a six-thirty pace!"

"I know!" he yelled back. "I know!"

At that moment I started crying. I wasn't the only one. Other fans around me were holding up signs, playing bongo drums, and screaming for their runners too. I believe that kind of enthusiasm is what David conveys in Psalm 9:1–4, a psalm that is passionate, excited, and ready to celebrate.

Of course, cheering on runners pales in comparison to celebrating the wonderful deeds of our heavenly Father. Yet, when I read the first few verses of Psalm 9, I couldn't help but think of a marathon crowd. The passion of marathon spectators and their enthusiasm is similar to David's, but the similarities don't end there. In this psalm, David announces that he will "recount all of [God's] wonderful deeds" (v. 1), and he praises God's gracious deeds throughout the psalm. David doesn't simply say "I love you" to God over and over. Rather, David thanks our heavenly Father for His individual blessings and truly praises Him not just for who He *is*, but also for what He *has done* for him.

As I've learned more about God over the years, my faith has changed, and my praise has changed too. Our God is dynamic and active for us. . . . God always surprises me by answering my prayers in wonderful ways I don't always expect.

When Mike ran past, I didn't just say "Yea! Go fast!" Because I love my husband and because I had learned and trained with him, I understood how exciting it was that he was running three minutes faster than planned. My cheering—my praise—was so much more personal and exciting because I really understood not only *who* Mike was but also *what* he was doing.

As I've learned more about God over the years, my faith has changed, and my praise has changed too. Our God is dynamic and active for us, and I join David when I "give thanks to the Lord with my whole heart; [and] I . . . recount all of [His] wonderful deeds" (v. 1). God always surprises me by answering my prayers in wonderful ways I don't always expect.

Christina

And yet, the more I understand who God is, the more I understand how miserable I would be without Him. In verse 3, David recognizes how depressing life as an unbeliever would be. His "enemies" are Gentiles, or unbelievers. When faced with the truth of a holy and righteous God, these people refuse to recognize their need for a Savior. So they "stumble and perish" in their sin.

Even after understanding God's wonderful deeds and how desperate I am for His grace, I still stumble in my own sin. I can be as sanctimonious as a Pharisee, announcing how much I love God while being ungrateful for what He has done. Or I begin to count God's wonderful deeds in my life as my own. Our Christian family? The product of my husband and me teaching good values in the home. Our financial success? The result of our hard work and careful investing. My Christian friends? The consequence of the loyalty and understanding I've shown them over the years.

I can continue thinking this way until I open the Bible and come face-to-face with the truth. I see who I am—a sinner—ready to "stumble" and "perish." And I see who God is—God the Most High (v. 2). But in God's Word I also see His wonderful deeds through His Son, Jesus Christ. Jesus obeyed the Law perfectly for me. While He hung on the cross, God declared Jesus guilty and me innocent, God's own "righteous judgment" (v. 4). God welcomed me into His family through Baptism, taking away my sins and giving me a good conscience (1 Peter 1:31–32). Now, I can once again "give thanks with my whole heart" (Psalm 9:1).

Despite both his training and my cheering, Mike still hasn't qualified for the Boston Marathon. But year after year, he gets another chance to race, and I get another chance to drag out my neon signs and megaphone.

You know, it really is a shame they stay in the closet until the local marathon every year. Maybe I should take them out for church this Sunday and pass them around as our congregation gives thanks to the Lord. Together, even if it's only in our hearts, we can jump up and down and recount God's wonderful deeds, indeed!

Christina

Prayer: Dear God, thank You for each of Your wonderful deeds. Help me see them in my daily life. Thank You for sending Your Son, Jesus, who redeemed me from my own stumbling. In His holy name. **Amen.**

Christina

monday

Personal Study Questions:
Psalm 9:1–4

1. Join the psalmist right now, taking a few moments to "recount all of [the LORD's] wonderful deeds." How have those wonderful deeds touched you . . .

   * Spiritually?
   * Physically?
   * Emotionally?
   * Intellectually?
   * Socially?

2. Underline the four "I wills" in verses 1–2. Some days we may feel thankful and glad; other days we may not. As the redeemed, sanctified people of the Lord Jesus, we need not allow our feelings to determine our response to God's goodness in our lives. We can rely on the Holy Spirit's work within us to turn our hearts to willing thanksgiving and gladness.

   a. Are you feeling particularly glad, exultant, or thankful right now? If so, praise Jesus for the wonderful deeds you listed in answer to question 1 above.

   b. Are you feeling less than fully glad, exultant, or thankful right now? If so, ask the Holy Spirit to work in you a whole-hearted response of willing praise to your Most High Redeemer-God, despite your mood.

3. How freeing to know we are not slaves to our emotional state! We can act as if we feel glad and confident, knowing that in any situation our good God—the God who gave His own Son into death for us—loves us and is indeed at work for our ultimate good. In what ways does this truth stir hope in your heart today?

Christina

21

Psalm 9:5–8

*The enemy came to an end in everlasting ruins;
their cities You rooted out; the very memory of them
has perished. But the LORD sits enthroned forever;
He has established His throne for justice.*

The War Won

If your household is like ours, the common cold is more like the constant cold, medicine is stashed in every bathroom cabinet, and the flu shot hardly combats the virus that moves in from September to May. And if you're household is like ours, you're also losing the war against the enemy: illness.

I had a painful fever blister on my lip my first day as a new teacher, a bad cold on my wedding day, and laryngitis the day my first book was published. These aren't merely unfortunate coincidences; my immune system is just weak. I understand what David means when he refers to "the wicked" (Psalm 9:5) and "everlasting ruins" (v. 6). My enemy may not be Goliath or the Philistines, but I've felt the endless ruin that comes from being sick.

Christina

My body loves to play hostess to pink eye, rotavirus, and stomach bugs. I try to combat these enemies by scrubbing my hands until they're chapped. I make eight hours of sleep a priority, and I drink as many glasses of water as my small bladder can hold. I disinfect our house as if it were a rest-stop bathroom in need of a good cleaning, and I would rather put a raw piece of chicken into my mouth than my own unsanitized finger.

Recently I read that church is among the germiest places because members attend even when they're sick. Of course, being surrounded by Christian friends is one of the many reasons I enjoy church. But I hadn't realized that on Sunday I might actually pick up an infection that would prohibit my activities the rest of the week. I feel David's passion in Psalm 9 when my Christian brothers and sisters and I join to recount God's wonderful deeds. But my love of worship and fear of germs collided when our twins were born six weeks early.

The NICU (neonatal intensive care unit) is a scary place for parents—their newborns attached to feeding tubes, heart monitors, and oxygen. The nurses teach you early that germs are trying to attack your precious babies and that you should be afraid, very afraid.

The neonatologists instructed my husband and me to scrub our hands, arms, and fingernails before, after, and in between touching our babies and to change our scrubs too. Our son and daughter couldn't come into contact with each other while in the NICU; they lay in separate Isolettes. When the twins were finally released from the hospital, the nursing staff warned us about possible infections by common germs. As preemies, their immune systems made mine look strong.

Our house became even more of a war zone—the battle lines were drawn, and disease was the clear enemy. We weren't quite as strict as the NICU had been, but we tried our best. Bottles of hand sanitizer were now on every coffee table and bookcase. The babies didn't leave the house, and our three-year-old knew to wash her hands every time she ran past the sink.

I dreaded taking Samuel and Elisabeth to church even a

Christina

23

couple months after their birth. I wanted to go so badly, but it felt too soon. I feared what could happen: we would share the peace with someone hosting walking pneumonia, one of the twins would come down with a 104-degree fever, both babies would be readmitted into the hospital, and it would all be my fault for taking them out too soon.

The twins' Baptisms worried me the most. In our family, Baptisms mean lots of out-of-town company and lots of baby holding. How could I invite all those germs into our home? On the other hand, at two months they were already weeks older than their big sister had been when she was baptized. Wasn't it time?

And as I looked into Sam's and Ellie's tiny faces, I knew they would be okay. Even if they got colds, or worse, a more epic battle had been won for them. These little miracles belonged to God forever, and no pink eye, chicken pox, cough, or cold would change that.

I remember when I finally realized that my lifelong fear of germs was really damaging my perspective. I was writing a Sunday School lesson about Baptism for junior high students. Trying to think of a creative way to teach about Baptism, I decided to include a war activity—after all, what sixth grader doesn't love running around yelling battle cries? I started by sharing the Law, which is always easy with junior high students. They are all too familiar with our unfair, difficult, depressing, and sinful world. As Christians, we are at odds with this world, fighting against sin, death, and the devil. But truth be told, we do a miserable job of it. Choosing to fight on our own, we always lose.

However, Jesus has already fought our enemies on His cross. His resurrection proves His victory! God has given us Baptism to unite us with Christ's death and resurrection and to adopt us into His holy family. Through faith in His Son, we are reunited with our heavenly Father, our Creator. Instantly we are winners. We have eternal life! We have eternal happiness! The battle against sin has been won!

It was as if God was whispering these words into my ear. God wanted to be reunited with these babies He had given us. He wanted them to join His family through Baptism. Trying to fight sin on my own by withholding this Sacrament from my twins was

Christina

completely backward. God wanted our babies to enjoy the blessings of forgiveness, eternal life, and eternal happiness available to them in this means of grace. David praised God for triumphing over the enemy: "You have rebuked the nations; You have made the wicked perish; You have blotted out their name forever and ever" (v. 5). God's triumphant work was done by Jesus on Calvary, and He was offering it to my family!

So, Sam and Ellie were baptized. Family and friends (some coughing, some sneezing) came to our house and held the babies. Sixty people crowded into our home and shared germs over prayers and praises and pink and blue cupcakes. As I looked into Sam's and Ellie's tiny faces, I knew they would be okay. Even if they got colds, or worse, a more epic battle had been won for them. These little miracles belonged to God forever, and no pink eye, chicken pox, cough, or cold would change that.

After all, as David declares, "The enemy came to an end in everlasting ruins; their cities you uprooted out; the very memory of them has perished. But the LORD sits enthroned forever; He has established His throne for justice" (Psalm 9:6–7). Jesus has triumphed over sin, death, and the devil's power. The victories of the Creator are our victories, those He created. The triumph of the Redeemer is the triumph of the redeemed!

Of course Sam and Ellie will still know sin and the results of sin in their lives. I can't protect them from their guilt when they disobey God's commands or from the sting of a loved one's death. But as David rejoices in verses 7–8, God's justice will always prevail. Jesus defeated our enemies on the cross, and by that He provides justice for all of us. God, who loves righteousness, has anointed all of us with the oil of joy (Hebrews 1:9).

Hallelujah, and bring on the celebration—germs and all!

Christina

Prayer: Heavenly Father, thank You for send-
ing Your Son, who won the war over sin. Thank
You for forgiving me when I forget that You have
already triumphed over all my enemies. Thank
You for giving me Your forgiving grace through
Your Word and Sacraments. In Jesus' name I pray.
Amen.

Christina

tuesday

Personal Study Questions: Psalm 9:5–8

1. Yesterday you underlined four "I wills." Now go back and underline the five "You haves" in verses 3–6.

   a. For what five "wonderful deeds" in particular does the psalmist, David, praise God?

   b. If you were to name five "You haves" from your own life, similar to those David mentions, which wonderful deeds of your mighty Savior-God would you list?

2. Because we know our sins, the "rebuke" of God (v. 5) could (and should!) frighten us. But how do God's wonderful deeds described in 2 Corinthians 5:19–21 calm those fears?

3. As long as we live here on earth, we will be at war, as today's faith narrative explains. Yet Jesus has won the victory for us. God's justice will prevail. Our chief enemies—sin, death, and the devil—have been defeated on the cross. Our Lord Jesus Christ sits enthroned as the righteous judge who enacts justice for His people. In what specific situations drawn from this week's world news or your own personal circumstances can this truth encourage you?

Christina

27

Psalm 9:9–12

*The L*ORD *is a stronghold for the oppressed,
a stronghold in times of trouble. And those who know Your
name put their trust in You, for You,
O L*ORD, *have not forsaken those who seek You.*

Our Stronghold

I have a passion for pictures. The perfect photograph, the kind that captures a moment, is priceless. Admittedly, to achieve perfection I've spent thousands of dollars and thousands of hours staging, snapping, and developing. Another problem with having a passion for pictures? After years of chasing the elusive perfect photograph, I have too many of them.

When our children were born, I was in awe of their innocence. To try to capture it on film, I spent a good chunk of time and our budget rushing to the drugstore for film, prints, and scrapbooks.

About the time I was elbow-deep in black film canisters, digital cameras became popular. Convenient and

Christina

28

cheap, no one was more thrilled than I at their arrival. Finally, I would be able to develop and print only the pictures I really liked—and I could just e-mail them to family and friends. We would save thousands of hours and even more dollars!

Five years later, I had enough untitled images on my computer's hard drive that I longed for twenty-four exposure film. I had fallen into a bad habit. When I uploaded images from my digital camera, I should have immediately sorted them into folders. Instead, I crammed them into a "New Pictures" folder. There were no "new" pictures in this folder, just old ones from my daughter's previous birthdays and everything in between. There were thousands of jpegs, and I had no idea what any of them were.

A friend who had just become a consultant for a scrapbook supply company told me, "You need to get organized! Don't take any more pictures until you sort through the ones crowding your hard drive. Name them, organize them, and print the ones you like. No more pictures until you get control!"

I took only her last bit of advice: I stopped taking pictures. I decided the whole thing was just too overwhelming. Unless friends and family members sent me actual prints, I didn't even detach jpegs from their e-mails. Why bother? These images would just end up in my computer wasteland, where they went to die. I felt like the oppressed David describes in Psalm 9:9: I was inundated with images, and I needed a stronghold.

Actually the pictures weren't oppressing me; it was my own sinful heart, the heart of a control freak. When I finally began to sort through the images stored on my computer, I realized I was trying to control time. I have dozens of pictures of us holding our twins about the time they started crawling, as if once they took off on their own, they'd never snuggle into our arms again. By capturing those moments, I was trying to delay the future. If my life were organized into scrapbook pages, perhaps I would be in total control. But it never worked that way. David praises God for hearing the "cry of the afflicted" in Psalm 9:12. My need for control was my affliction.

Christina

That affliction snuck into everything I did. I saw the ugly side of my control-freakiness when I began graduate school. My first class, a creative-writing workshop, had only one Christian student: me. As we wrote and shared our poetry, short stories, and plays, I learned about the drama in my classmates' lives. Creative writing is inherently personal, and writers reveal a lot of their lives through their stories and poetry. My classmates' writings were filled with debauchery, revenge, and sadness. I wanted more and more to help these dejected men and women. They were oppressed and afflicted in a completely desperate way: they didn't know they needed a Savior. Through conversations about their writing, I learned that many of them had long ago rejected Jesus. He was just a punch line to their jokes, a symbol of a life they had given up, His name a mere curse word on their lips.

Through my poetry and our conversations, I was delighted to sing God's praises to those men and women. As I did, I learned that my classmates were searching. In most cases, they were anxious to learn about Jesus. I prayed for each of them and asked God to show them the forgiveness, holiness, and completeness that was theirs through faith in His Son, Jesus Christ.

I wanted to share the Gospel with them, but I wasn't sure how. I considered inviting them to church with me or doing some mass evangelism with an announcement during class. But to my control-freak nature, all that seemed too overwhelming. Once I got started, where would sharing the Gospel end? Right outside our classroom were crowds of people—some of them Muslim, some Hindu, some Jewish. I could witness to one person or even a group in my class, but there would still be thousands more desperate for the Gospel of Jesus Christ. And every day—every hour—hundreds more were falling away from their Creator, falling away from their Savior. The whole thing felt as impossible and unmanageable as all those unnamed images on my computer. Better to give up than frustrate myself by starting something I could never finish.

Of course, that was the point. I could never save a single person because I wasn't their Savior. Just as I learned that I could

Christina

30

never control time through photography, I cannot control the hearts of others or create faith in them. In a sermon, our pastor explained 1 Corinthians 12. When I heard the words "no one can say 'Jesus is Lord' except in the Holy Spirit" (v. 3), I realized that I hadn't entrusted God with my classmates' spiritual welfare. I hadn't even prayed for them. How ironic! I wanted to share God's love and grace in Jesus Christ, but I hadn't asked Him for help.

Like Psalm 9:10 proclaims, I put my trust in God, and He did not forsake me. Through my writing, I shared with my classmates the wonderful deeds that verse 11 praises Him for—the escape from sin and sadness God provides through His Son. I could rejoice with David's praise in Psalm 9:9–11, "The LORD is a stronghold for the oppressed, a stronghold in times of trouble. And those who know Your name put their trust in You, for You, LORD, have never forsaken those who seek You. Sing praises to the LORD, who sits enthroned in Zion! Tell among the peoples His deeds!" God had not forsaken me, and for Christ's sake He would not forsake others who sought Him in repentant faith.

Through my poetry and our conversations, I was delighted to sing God's praises to those men and women. As I did, I learned that my classmates were searching. In most cases, they were anxious to learn about Jesus. I prayed for each of them and asked God to show them the forgiveness, holiness, and completeness that was theirs through faith in His Son, Jesus Christ.

David rejoices, "He does not forget the cry of the afflicted" (v. 12). Thank the Lord that despite my need for control, He presses on with His perfect plan. Praise the Lord that it's not our responsibility to control the spread of His Gospel any more than it's our job to freeze time in photographs. In the loving and capable arms of our Savior, we are His. He will never forsake us. "The Lord is a stronghold for the oppressed, a stronghold in times of trouble"(v. 9). Let us sing His praises to the world, which needs our gracious Savior!

Christina

31

Prayer: Dear God, heavenly Father, my sinful heart wants to control every part of my life. Help me to see that You are my stronghold, that You will never forsake me. Help me to share Your miraculous grace and Your wonderful deeds with others. In the name of Jesus, my Savior. **Amen.**

Christina

wednesday

Personal Study Questions: Psalm 9:9–12

1. In what ways do you fight the same battle for control described by today's faith narrative? In what ways is this a sin against the First Commandment—the Lord's command that we have no other gods?

2. Reread verse 10. Compare it with Proverbs 18:10. What names of God revealed in Scripture bring you special comfort when you run to your Lord, trusting Him for pardon, help, and safety in times of need? How can these help when you're tempted to wrench control away from your heavenly Father?

3. The last part of verse 12 promises that our God "does not forget the cry of the afflicted."

   a. For what are you crying out to God right now?

   b. When has it seemed as though He has forgotten you or as if He may be ignoring you?

   c. How does the promise of verse 12 help in view of Satan's temptation to unbelief or even despair?

Christina

Psalm 9:13–16

Be gracious to me, O LORD! See my affliction from those who hate me, O You who lift me up from the gates of death, that I may recount all Your praises, that in the gates of the daughter of Zion I may rejoice in Your salvation.

You Lift Me Up

As a mother, one of the highest points in my life was also one of the lowest. This occurred when I drove my car past our house, saw was what was happening there, crouched down, and hid. I didn't cry, but a feeling of defeat spread throughout my body. I clenched my eyes shut so I wouldn't fall apart.

No, my home had not been invaded by terrorists nor was it being repossessed by the bank. To be honest, the situation was bizarre. We had invited all those people to

Christina

our house and were paying them a lot of money to be there.

Let me explain. About seven months earlier, I learned I was pregnant with twins. Our oldest daughter had just turned two and was thriving. Our lives felt very full. The idea of adding two newborns to our household seemed overwhelming to say the least.

Unfortunately, everyone else agreed. As I became as big as house, every cashier, bank teller, and church member remarked that I must be having twins. People asked how I would be able to handle everything. One woman in a discount store checkout line even tried to convince me that I was unable to handle two babies at once.

Being pragmatic people, my husband and I made a plan: we decided to secure outside help. We already knew that the first few months with a newborn are exhausting. In order to give two babies and a young child the care they needed, we would trim our schedules. Mike enjoyed mowing the lawn, but a company could do that. I didn't enjoy housecleaning, so we found someone to do that. When my doctor instructed me to stay off my feet, we also realized we needed a nanny.

We prayed for good help, and God gave us a wonderful Christian nanny. At the end of my pregnancy, when I experienced around-the-clock contractions, every pair of extra hands was put to use. Then the babies came early, by C-section, and had to stay in the hospital for a couple of weeks. I struggled with postpartum depression and was still on painkillers from the surgery, so I couldn't drive on my own to visit them. The help, plus the extra hands of our families, was needed.

Six weeks later, about the time of the twins' actual due date, everything turned around. The babies were sleeping regularly, our oldest daughter had settled firmly into her big sister role, and I had recovered from surgery. I was feeling great. Caring for newborn twins and a three-year-old wasn't so daunting, but what was becoming unbearable was all that help crowding around us.

Which brings me to that dark moment as I drove by our house. The lawn crew was picking up after our dog, the housekeeper was probably inside scrubbing our floors, and it was about

Christina

naptime for the twins, so the nanny was surely rocking them to sleep. All the planning Mike and I had done to handle the birth of the twins was working out perfectly. Only suddenly, it was all so oppressive.

This certainly wasn't the "gates of death" David describes in verse 13, and I know that too much help at home sounds like a silly problem to have. However, after months of lying around gestating and recovering, I was tired of asking others to take care of my family. I knew that I couldn't spend the twins' infanthood hiding in the car, struggling to find my place among all that help.

Sure, there was a trail of white spit-up down my shoulder, Sam was wearing a pink bib, and Ellie's bib said, "I'm the little brother," but we had made it out of the house! Knowing that God was working a miracle through me gave me confidence, and who was I to argue with the Provider?

That night, Mike and I prayed for a solution to reclaim our house and kids. The very next day, our nanny told us that her husband had accepted a job at a church in California and they would move in a couple of weeks. Fall had arrived, and our lawn didn't need to be mowed as often. And the housekeeper? Well, the housekeeper we would employ only once a week.

Mike and I asked God to give me energy to handle the sleeplessness, serenity to handle the pressure of three little people's needs, and discretion to organize the chaotic days of the five of us, not including the dog—I can't forget the constantly barking dog!—until Mike got home from work each day to share the work with me.

I knew there were trying moments to come and I was ready for them. Surprisingly, the most trying moments didn't come from the kids, they came from strangers—like those standing in a checkout line—staring at our stroller bulging with two babies and Catie, twirling around and chattering to me. Yes, it could all feel overwhelming when one of the twins didn't nurse and preferred to scream like only an infant can. Or when Catie didn't nap and preferred to scream like only a three-year-old can. But I like to think I handled all that like only a mother can.

But we were doing fine. We really were! When I left the

Christina

house, I felt empowered, in love with my family, and like this was the most exciting time of my life. Sure, there was a trail of white spit-up down my shoulder, Sam was wearing a pink bib, and Ellie's bib said, "I'm the little brother," but we had made it out of the house! Knowing that God was working a miracle through me gave me confidence, and who was I to argue with the Provider?

However, after a few months, I found that I preferred anything to listening to strangers with perfectly good intentions tell me they were concerned that I find help. I didn't have time to explain that I had employed a household of help and now was choosing to do it this way. I tried to respond, "God has blessed us," but the strangers looked at me like I was crazy. Like David, I prayed for God's mercy and for Him to lift me up (v. 13). And He did.

Of course, those who told me we couldn't manage without their idea of assistance were only human. As much as I disliked their remarks, as much as I knew their comments would be "snared in the work of their own hands" (v. 16), I also knew that God would continue to bless my family—and, prayerfully, these strategies—with the ability to trust Him. In Christ, "the Lord has made Himself known" (v. 16): He has revealed His heart of love and forgiveness. God made Himself known every day, not just through the blessings of energy and serenity He gave me, but especially through the work of our Savior—the most important work of all. My prayer now included those who said we could not manage our lives by ourselves, that they would see our excitement as a witness to God's most precious work of all.

Like He gave to David, God had given me the opportunity to "recount all [His] praises, that in the gates of the daughter of Zion I may rejoice in [His] salvation" (v. 14). Through faith in Christ, our chaotic lives can be a testimony that God provides and that through Him, nothing is impossible. So do not despair. Whether you are at a high point in you life or at a low, or somewhere in between, He will lift you up!

Christina

Prayer: Dear God, thank You for Your endless blessings. Make my life a testimony of Your goodness and the gift of Your Son. Help me to trust You in every part of my life. In Jesus' name. Amen.

Christina

thursday

Personal Study Questions:
Psalm 9:13–16

1. Notice that verse 13 personalizes and specifically defines the promise of verse 12. How so?

2. What "gates" in verse 13 contrast with those in verse 14?

3. When have you experienced the Lord's rescue from "the gates of death" and, as a result, been enabled to recount His praises in "the gates of the daughter of Zion," the company of the faithful, the Holy Christian Church? (Your examples need not be dramatic. Consider the story from today's faith narrative as you think about situations from your own life.)

Christina

Psalm 9:17–20

*The wicked shall return to Sheol, all the nations that
forget God. For the needy shall not always be forgotten,
and the hope of the poor shall not perish forever.*

Pride of Place

In the last four verses of Psalm 9, David sounds a little battle-worn, doesn't he? He calls his people "needy" and "poor" (v. 18). He seems exasperated with the other godless nations that have been fighting Israel. He calls them "wicked" and "nations that forget God" (v. 17). In verse 19, he asks God to judge them, and he ends the psalm with verse 20: "Put them in fear, O LORD! Let the nations know that they are but men!" Seems a little harsh, doesn't it?

Looking closer at the psalm, I realized that David is writing not just as a believer but also as a king who has a lot at stake with Israel's neighbors. To put it in modern terms, David was fighting for bragging rights—for God. Calling on God to help the Israelites in battle was evange-

Christina

40

lism. The other countries would understand that if Israel was the strongest nation, it was because they had the strongest God.

Asking God to "let the nations know that they are but men!" was asking Him to squelch those other countries' pride in their false gods and show them who they were without the true God. David's pride in our God inspires me. And I'm a Texan, so I know a thing or two about pride—only the pride I'm talking about is for our state.

Here in Houston there's a DJ who ends his daily show with the request, "Folks, won't you take some time today and thank God that you're a Texan?" That's how they talk on country music stations in Texas. Perhaps sharing this bit of Texas pride will help you understand the loyalty citizens have for our state. I'm not defending arrogance. I'm just acknowledging that if you're in Texas, there is serious pressure to be proud this state is your birthplace/family's birthplace/vacation spot/place you moved for work.

My parents fell into the last category after they accepted calls to teach in Galveston. My mom, an umpteenth-generation Midwesterner, is from a large farming family in Minnesota. My dad, who loves the blue skies and mountains of the southwest, is from New Mexico. Birthing and raising Texans was not necessarily in their life plans. What about me? Enough years of Go Texan Day, studying Texas history in school, reciting the Texas pledge (no, I'm not kidding), and reading Texas-pride bumper stickers, and I fell deeply in love with the Lone Star State.

And if you'll just allow one further bit of devotion, I have to ask: what's not to love? The state includes most every type of geography. The food, whether it's barbeque, Tex-Mex, or seafood, is delicious. The people—well, they're friendly, hospitable, and passionate.

With this kind of sentiment when I went to college in Nebraska, I missed my home state so much that I was never really interested in finding out what Nebraska offered. I remember only that the people were nice and that the winters were cold. I admit now that after I graduated I was more concerned with getting back to Texas than I was with going to Cornhusker football

Christina

games or visiting the state capitol.

I did move back home to Texas, except I didn't leave quite as no-strings-attached as I had planned. A month before I moved away, I fell in love with a born, bred, bleeds-Cornhusker-red Nebraska boy. We married the following year, and he agreed to live in Texas. While I am a first-generation Texan, Mike's entire family is Nebraskan. Not only is every generation of his family tree from Lancaster County, they love the state, they celebrate its history, they are involved in local politics, and they can't imagine why anyone would live anywhere else. Yes, they are almost as proud to be Nebraskans as Texans are to be Texans.

Despite Mike's love for his home, he embraced the South. He listened to my friends as they bragged about Texas (did you know that the first word spoken from the moon was "Houston"?), he ate Tex-Mex six times a week, and he even told people that the warm weather was a nice change.

So, of course, I did the same. Our first Thanksgiving, we traveled to Nebraska and watched the Huskers play at Memorial Stadium. It was at that game that I had the long-overdue realization that Texans are not the only ones with near-obsessive loyalty. When the team ran onto the field through the "Tunnel Walk" and Tom Osborne joined them, the sea of red swelled with hysteria. As I looked around at the cheering, screaming faces, I finally understood that my state wasn't the greatest, it was just mine. I began to really pay attention to my husband's home. Fall in the Midwest *is* beautiful—the Technicolor leaves; the crisp, dry air; the clear, blue skies; and families (all dressed in Cornhusker red) playing football in front yards. Back home, everyone was doing their Christmas shopping in shorts and complaining about the humidity. I felt a little like a Texas traitor (and according to Texas history, we hate traitors), but I could see that other places can be just as good as the Lone Star State.

In Psalm 9:19, David asks God to judge the other nations who were struggling with pride—but of the sinister kind. I can

Jesus shows me that because of His redeeming love, I can be needy and poor. Through Jesus' cross and empty tomb, God has proven He will not forget people like me nor allow my hope to perish (v. 18).

Christina

imagine David shaking his head at those godless countries, saddened by their loyalty to empty, fake gods. Their pride—devoted to something so meaningless—was wasted.

Maybe you can relate. I admit that self-pride is the sin that stunts my Christian growth the most. When David rejoices with the "poor" and "needy" in verse 18, I have trouble relating. I know that Christians who are poor and needy in spirit are blessed (remember the "Blessed are you's" of Matthew 5:3–12?). But I have trouble admitting I need anyone or anything, let alone that I'm so worthless I need a Savior to rescue me from myself.

Thankfully, God's grace extends even to sinners like me. I pray that God will continue to show me how blinding my self-pride truly is. Left on my own, I could be just like those nations in Psalm 9 and wallow in my own pride. But because of Jesus, I don't have to. When my self-pride blinds me, He opens my eyes through faith. Jesus shows me that because of His redeeming love, I can be needy and poor. Through Jesus' cross and empty tomb, God has proven He will not forget people like me nor allow my hope to perish (v. 18).

Oh, and that state pride thing? For now, my husband and I are raising our children in Texas. Yes, our kids are constantly inundated with all things Texas, but they see the rest of the world too. I sure am glad that we travel to the Midwest several times a year and that their grandparents are teaching them what a world away from home has to offer.

I have to be honest: there are still some days that I take that DJ's advice and thank God that He made me a Texan. But even more, every day I thank Him that He made me His daughter through faith in His Son.

Christina

Prayer: Dear God, thank You for sending Your Son to win the war against sin. Humble me so I can see how poor and needy I am for Your redemption. Give me the words to tell our pride-filled world the Good News about Your Son. In Jesus' name. **Amen.**

Christina

Friday

Personal Study Questions:
Psalm 9:17–20

1. In verses 11–20, we see that David's "I wills" of praise and exaltation from verses 1–2 did not grow out of a peaceful, trouble-free time in life. What evidence of trouble and turmoil can you find in the last two-thirds of the psalm?

2. Reread verses 1–2 in light of this. What new insights do you gain as you consider both the praises and the problems the psalm describes?

3. While no one knows for sure, some scholars believe the word *Selah* refers to a musical interlude timed in such a way as to allow worshipers to pause and meditate on the truths just shared by the choir. In that sense, *Selah* may mean, "Pause and think about this." The two *Selahs* in Psalm 9 (following vv. 16 and 20) invite us to pause and consider the Spirit-inspired truths recorded here. Do that right now. What new hope and thankfulness spring from your "whole heart" (v. 1) as a result?

Christina

Group Bible Study for Week One
Psalm 9

1. If you were to choose one verse from Psalm 9 to memorize as a result of your study this past week, which verse would you pick? Why?

2. As David prays verses 1–3, we might get the impression he does so from a trouble-free sanctuary. Yet the verses that follow make it clear he has more than his share of trouble and difficulty.

    a. Share with the group the evidence of turmoil you see in the psalm.

    b. What insights did you glean from your study this week regarding the interplay between our emotions and our faith?

    c. How could we help friends caught in the feelings-faith paradox?

3. The "heart" in Scripture refers not so much to our emotions but rather to those core beliefs, attitudes, and values we hold most dear. How could knowing this encourage you to join David's "I wills," his words of praise despite his feelings?

4. Verse 7 begins with the word "but," indicating a contrast. How do verses 5–6 contrast sharply with verses 7–8?

5. Read Psalm 9:10 and Proverbs 18:10 aloud.

   a. Work with your group to list as many names for God revealed in Scripture as you can recall.

   b. What does each name tell you about Him?

   c. How or when could each of the names comfort, encourage, or embolden you?

   d. With all that in mind, why are these passages such powerful and uplifting promises?

6. Which faith narratives from this past week brought the truths of Psalm 9 home to you in a particularly meaningful way? Share your observations with your group.

7. Keeping the truths of Psalm 9 in mind, what praises and thanksgivings would you like to include in your prayers as today's Bible study session concludes? For what blessings would you like to ask? Make lists together, and then talk to your Lord about His "wonderful deeds," past, present, and future, before each of you go your separate ways.

Week Two

Psalm 18

¹ I love You, O LORD, my strength.

² The LORD is my rock and my fortress and my
deliverer,
my God, my rock, in whom I take refuge,
my shield, and the horn of my salvation, my
stronghold.

³ I call upon the LORD, who is worthy to be
praised,
and I am saved from my enemies.

⁴ The cords of death encompassed me;
the torrents of destruction assailed me;

⁵ the cords of Sheol entangled me;
the snares of death confronted me.

⁶ In my distress I called upon the LORD;
to my God I cried for help.
From His temple He heard my voice,
and my cry to Him reached His ears.

⁷ Then the earth reeled and rocked;
the foundations also of the mountains trembled
and quaked, because He was angry.

⁸ Smoke went up from His nostrils,
and devouring fire from His mouth;
glowing coals flamed forth from Him.

⁹ He bowed the heavens and came down;
thick darkness was under His feet.

¹⁰ He rode on a cherub and flew;
He came swiftly on the wings of the wind.

¹¹ He made darkness His covering, His canopy
around Him,
thick clouds dark with water.

¹² Out of the brightness before Him
hailstones and coals of fire broke through His
clouds.

¹³ The LORD also thundered in the heavens,
and the Most High uttered His voice,
hailstones and coals of fire.

¹⁴ And He sent out His arrows and scattered them;
He flashed forth lightnings and routed them.

¹⁵ Then the channels of the sea were seen,
and the foundations of the world were laid bare
at Your rebuke, O LORD,
at the blast of the breath of Your nostrils.

¹⁶ He sent from on high, He took me;
He drew me out of many waters.

¹⁷ He rescued me from my strong enemy
and from those who hated me,
for they were too mighty for me.

¹⁸ They confronted me in the day of my calamity,
but the LORD was my support.

¹⁹ He brought me out into a broad place;
He rescued me, because He delighted in me.

²⁰ The LORD dealt with me according to my
righteousness;
according to the cleanness of my hands He re-
warded me.

²¹ For I have kept the ways of the LORD,
and have not wickedly departed from my God.

²² For all His rules were before me,
and His statutes I did not put away from me.

²³ I was blameless before Him,
and I kept myself from my guilt.

²⁴ So the LORD has rewarded me according to my righteousness,
according to the cleanness of my hands in His sight.

²⁵ With the merciful You show Yourself merciful;
with the blameless man You show Yourself blameless;

²⁶ with the purified You show Yourself pure;
and with the crooked You make Yourself seem tortuous.

²⁷ For You save a humble people,
but the haughty eyes You bring down.

²⁸ For it is You who light my lamp;
the LORD my God lightens my darkness.

²⁹ For by You I can run against a troop,
and by my God I can leap over a wall.

³⁰ This God—His way is perfect;
the word of the LORD proves true;
He is a shield for all those who take refuge in Him.

³¹ For who is God, but the LORD?
And who is a rock, except our God?—

³² the God who equipped me with strength
and made my way blameless.

³³ He made my feet like the feet of a deer
and set me secure on the heights.

³⁴ He trains my hands for war,
so that my arms can bend a bow of bronze.

³⁵ You have given me the shield of Your salvation,
and Your right hand supported me,
and Your gentleness made me great.

³⁶ You gave a wide place for my steps under me,
and my feet did not slip.

³⁷ I pursued my enemies and overtook them,
and did not turn back till they were consumed.

³⁸ I thrust them through, so that they were not able to rise;
they fell under my feet.

³⁹ For You equipped me with strength for the battle;
You made those who rise against me sink under me.

⁴⁰ You made my enemies turn their backs to me,
and those who hated me I destroyed.

⁴¹ They cried for help, but there was none to save;
they cried to the LORD, but He did not answer them.

⁴² I beat them fine as dust before the wind;
I cast them out like the mire of the streets.

⁴³ You delivered me from strife with the people;
You made me the head of the nations;
people whom I had not known served me.

⁴⁴ As soon as they heard of me they obeyed me;
foreigners came cringing to me.

⁴⁵ Foreigners lost heart
and came trembling out of their fortresses.

⁴⁶ The LORD lives, and blessed be my rock,
and exalted be the God of my salvation—

⁴⁷ the God who gave me vengeance
and subdued peoples under me,

⁴⁸ who delivered me from my enemies;
yes, You exalted me above those who rose against me;
You rescued me from the man of violence.

⁴⁹ For this I will praise You, O LORD, among the nations,
and sing to Your name.

⁵⁰ Great salvation He brings to His king,
and shows steadfast love to His anointed,
to David and His offspring forever.

Lisa Hahn

Psalm 18:1–12

I call upon the LORD, who is worthy to be praised,
and I am saved from my enemies.

God's Daughter

My dad was 6' 2½" and weighed in at a fit 195 pounds. He worked as a lineman climbing utility poles, operating heavy equipment, and fixing downed power lines. At home, he was always busy with some repair or exciting new project. With his strong frame, huge hands, and seemingly endless inter-

lisa

ests and skills, I figured my dad could do or fix just about anything.

When he had a playhouse built in our yard, it wasn't just big enough for our dolls and us; fitted with sliding glass windows, it could easily sleep eight! When he built a deer stand, it was more like a watchtower—completely enclosed, also with windows, perched atop four 35-foot power poles. When our fifteen-year-old dog became sick, my dad built a casket—for use when the time came—big enough for Winkie's bed. It was lined with new red carpet, and the grooved wood was stained walnut brown. Huge hands plus a huge heart always equaled huge results!

Everyone knew my dad. No matter where he took my sister and me—the auto parts store, the feed store, or seemingly anywhere else in our small north-Wisconsin town—my dad knew somebody. I loved it when people would comment, "So, you must be Bernie's daughter."

I felt safe being Bernie's daughter. For while everyone was familiar with his jovial, fun-loving side . . . well . . . there was also another side. One evening we had a guest who was deeply involved in a non-Christian religion. My dad had made it clear to him that he was welcome in our home as long as he didn't "talk religion." As the evening wore on—you guessed it—this guest talked religion. The picture of my dad at that moment is best described in verse 8 of our psalm: "Smoke went up from His nostrils, and devouring fire from His mouth." Our guest was firmly and promptly escorted out the back door, through the garage, and straight to his car. I remember feeling a little afraid at that time, but mostly very safe and protected. Evil entered our home, and Daddy threw it out!

When I went to college, got my first job, and saw my dad less frequently, being Bernie's daughter now meant lots of encouraging letters and phone calls. It meant a folded ten-dollar bill pressed into my hand as I went out the door. He'd hug me, wink, and whisper with feigned secrecy, "Now don't tell Mom!" And always, without fail, I heard these words: "If you need anything, call Daddy." While this implied that I was still his little girl, I knew it also

Lisa

meant that at a moment's notice he would do whatever he could to help, encourage, and protect me.

Your story may be similar. Perhaps not. Not everyone grows up with a loving, protecting earthly father. We may not share similar memories of our earthly dads, but we do share the same heavenly Father! He is a Father who loves us perfectly, who is with us 24/7, and who knows and meets even our most specific needs. David calls Him our Rock, our Deliverer, our Shield, our Stronghold, and the Horn of our salvation.

So to rescue us, God's Son parted the heavens and came down (v. 9). He took on flesh and blood in the Virgin Mary's womb. Jesus' weakness at the cross was God's complete and perfect power over sin, death, and Satan. Jesus rose to seal eternal victory.

So we are the Rock's daughters—children of the Fortress. At our Baptism, we were declared daughters of the Deliverer, and when we call upon Him, we are saved from our enemies (v. 3). Who are our enemies? Let's make it easy by starting with sin, death, and Satan. Now let's get more specific: an untamed tongue, covetous thoughts, the desire to please, the need to feel indispensable, the desire to prove my point, addictions, and pride. Can you think of other "cords of death" or "torrents of destruction" (v. 4) that you may be dealing with?

Okay, now we have a list of sins, enemies to be thwarted. Let's "call upon the Lord" to save us. He has promised to hear our words of repentance and to forgive and renew us for the sake of His Son. Here comes our heavenly Father reaching down to save us, His beloved daughters, from the snares of eternal death! God's perfect love always has perfect results. But watch out, sin and death! Be ready for your world to shake because you will burn in defeat! According to our psalm, God's deliverance will be no small production because He is saving us from our enemies.

Sin and Satan do not go down easily, nor do our sinful natures. Have you ever vowed to conquer a specific sin that plagues you, say gossip? Isn't that just when you hear about something juicy you're just dying to share? Maybe you've resolved to speak more highly of your husband, and the break-room topic that week is "Typical Shortcomings of our Spouses"—wow, could you add fuel to that fire. Maybe you are determined to quit watching a less-than-appropriate television show, but this week they're airing the one key episode you missed last fall.

When we honestly confront our sin, we realize we cannot save ourselves. So when our cry for help reaches our heavenly Father's ears, creation reels and rocks (v. 7). As God comes to rescue us, the psalmist gives us a picture of smoke, fire, hail, and earthquakes (vv. 7–12). In other words, to conquer this enemy, it takes much more power than you or I will ever have!

Have you ever tried to rescue yourself with self-help books, denial, putting up a great facade, or sheer willpower? None of these attempts can match sin. So, to rescue us, God's Son parted the heavens and came down (v. 9). He took on flesh and blood in the Virgin Mary's womb. Jesus' weakness at the cross was God's complete and perfect power over sin, death, and Satan. Jesus rose to seal eternal victory. Now we receive His flesh and blood in the Sacrament of the Altar. Sin is defeated again, forgiveness is bestowed, and the pastor tells us to go in peace. The rescue is complete. Talk about huge results!

You are fully forgiven, fully equipped. As the cords of death try to choke you back into believing that they can hold you in your sin, call to your Father—your Rock—He is there to thwart, defeat, forgive, and equip, without fail.

Being Bernie's daughter was a tremendous blessing. I knew that while my dad was on this earth he would do anything within his power to help me. Knowing that I could "call Daddy" anytime gave me a constant sense of security. And I was so proud to belong to such a one-of-a-kind dad.

But being the Rock's daughter is even better. Being recognized as a child of God has great perks: I am forgiven in Christ, and I can call on Him daily to rescue me from my enemies. I know He will never leave me or forsake me (Joshua 1:5). I can tell others about God's forgiveness in my life, and I can forgive those who have wronged me (Romans 4:7–8). In my Baptism, I am God's daughter, and the promise of eternal life is mine (Galatians 3:26–29).

Lisa

God's daughter. That is who you are. Forgiven, rescued, pro-tected, redeemed. You are His. If you need anything . . . just call!

Prayer: Father, You are worthy to be praised. I deserve nothing but Your wrath, yet You call me Your child and reach down to rescue me from my sin again and again. In Christ, You give me victory. Thank You that I am Yours. In Jesus' name. **Amen.**

Lisa

monday

Personal Study Questions: Psalm 18:1–12

1. The title of Psalm 18 sets it in context. Although the titles of the Psalms are not considered part of the divinely inspired manuscript, still they are usually reliable and helpful. What do you learn from the title of Psalm 18 about the occasion that evoked David's worshipful response?

2. Circle all the "my"s in verses 1–2. What significant meaning does this use of personal pronouns add to the psalm? How does today's faith narrative help you make this connection?

3. In verses 4–15, David summarizes the Lord's saving help. Reread those words.

    a. What clues tell you a fierce thunderstorm may have blown in while David composed this part of the psalm?

    b. In what ways is God's deliverance like a storm?

lisa

Psalm 18:13–19

*He rescued me from my strong enemy and from those
who hated me, for they were too mighty for me.*

Just like Nell

Every Saturday morning it was the same hopeless scene: Nell Fenwick lay across the railroad tracks, bound tightly with rope by the dreadful Snidely Whiplash, train whistle in the distance, sounding nearer with each blast. Then, without fail, entered Dudley Do-Right. Confident, smiling, strong, and sure, with trademark cartoon-character ease, he'd rescue Nell just in the nick of time as the train whooshed past.

Now that I've sufficiently dated myself, let me explain. I used to dream of being rescued by a Dudley Do-

Lisa

56

Right. The excitement of having a brush with death only to be saved at just the right moment by a strong hero sounded great to me. While some little girls would never dream of allowing themselves to be captured in the first place, and some (my own daughter included) are confident that they could whip any villain on their own, a good old-fashioned rescue was always a part of my little girl daydreams.

I often acted out similar scenes with my dolls. Our poor little dog was subjected to my Nell-inspired play as well. My sister and I would be the bad guys and put Winkie under an inverted laundry basket. Then we'd return as the good guys and free him. One day we upgraded our prison from laundry basket to our small bedroom closet. Mom called us for lunch, and it was quite a while later before the good guys remembered to rescue Winkie.

Fortunately for me, little girl dreams never have become reality! Danger does not lurk around the corner each time I walk out the front door. I've never been tied to the railroad tracks. And while I have a wonderful husband, he has never had to fight off a villain to save me. At least not yet!

But God has! "He rescued me from my strong enemy and from those who hated me, for they were too mighty for me" (v. 17). Think about your worst enemies—the sins you can't seem to shake. Think about what most often makes you feel tied to the railroad tracks, helpless and hopeless. Is it impatience with your children manifested in a tone of voice that seems to have become the norm rather than the exception? Is it negative thoughts about someone you know that have come to define for you what type of a person he or she is? Is it the temptation to spend too much time out of the real world and in the fantasy world of a television show or virtual game? We can easily continue this list in our own minds. We are weighed down by occasional or habitual sins that are painfully obvious to those around us, as well as by sins we wouldn't dream of mentioning aloud or admitting to anyone.

In fact, we may not even be in the habit of admitting them to God and calling on Him to rescue us. Or we excuse some of our favorite sins as we willingly lie in the train's path by declaring,

"I'm just the type of person who likes to say what's on my mind—I can't help it if it hurts someone else" or "I just do not like conflict, so I am not going to bring it up" or "I can't help it that I _____; it runs in my family." We decide it isn't so bad being tied to those tracks—we can get up when we need to—and we become content with not being rescued at all. Or we may buy into the lie that we really do have our sin in check, that it's not all that bad, and that we can fight our own battles.

We are not in control. Someone else must defeat the enemy that is "too mighty for us." The train of eternal death is speeding toward us as we lie there, helpless. Just like Nell Fenwick tied to the tracks by Snidely Whiplash, we desperately need a hero. And then, without fail, enters Jesus.

After all, we live in a world that encourages self-reliance. Walk into any home improvement store and listen to the advertisements played over the loudspeakers. Watch a video demo on waterproofing your basement or replacing your bathtub. Within a short time, you will find your cart full of supplies and your head full of confidence that you, too, can complete what sounds like a simple weekend project.

About a year ago, while my kids and I were visiting Grandma, my husband called to ask what type of mirror or cabinet I wanted above the bathroom sink. For some time we had been planning to knock out plaster, hang drywall, lower the ceiling, install a fan, and basically create an entirely new bathroom. He was planning to surprise me and complete a large part of this project by the time I returned home at the end of the week. Long story short—we just hung that mirror about a month ago. Even with all of my husband's experience and skill, the fact is that remodeling takes time, money, and help from friends to whom we are forever grateful. Although from toddlerhood we encourage self-reliance with applause for "I did it all by myself" accomplishments and we all like a pat on the back for a job well done, we are far from being self sufficient—especially when it comes to defeating our sin.

The truth is, we are tied to the tracks, the train whistle is sounding louder, and we *do* need rescuing. But we *can't* do it ourselves. We are not in control. Someone else must defeat the enemy that is "too mighty for us." The train of eternal death is speeding

lisa

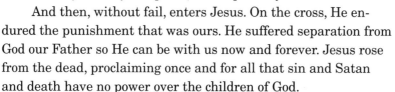

toward us as we lie there, helpless. Just like Nell Fenwick tied to the tracks by Snidely Whiplash, we desperately need a hero.

And then, without fail, enters Jesus. On the cross, He endured the punishment that was ours. He suffered separation from God our Father so He can be with us now and forever. Jesus rose from the dead, proclaiming once and for all that sin and Satan and death have no power over the children of God.

In our psalm, we have an awesome picture of God's power and wrath against our enemy. God's righteous anger causes creation to erupt with fury. And we have the vivid picture of God scooping us out of harm's way and drawing us up to safety. Notice that we do nothing. We are completely passive in this rescue operation. God gathers us to Himself so He can manifest His glory. He puts His helpless children in a safe place so we will be out of danger as He destroys our enemy. He holds back nothing as He shoots lightning bolts, rolls back the sea, and thunders His voice. The wickedness of our enemy is rendered powerless.

So I guess my dream of being snatched from the jaws of death like Nell Fenwick isn't such a fantasy after all. Not only have we been heroically saved from death, we have been brought "out into a broad place" (v. 19). The ropes of sin that immobilized us are no more. Unlike Nell's weekly dilemma, though, our rescue was a one-time, perfectly complete event. We are free forever to live and serve and thank our mighty God for all His goodness to us in Christ. Our hero!

Prayer: Heavenly Father, some days it seems I am bound by my worst enemies. Help me to recall how You won the victory over sin through Your Son's death and resurrection. Thank You for delighting in me, choosing me, and for the newness that comes each morning as I awake, Your baptized and forgiven child. In my Savior's name I pray. *Amen.*

Lisa

tuesday

Personal Study Questions:
Psalm 18:13–19

1. What sins most often cause you to feel that you, like Nell in the Dudley Do-Right cartoon, have been "tied to the railroad tracks" and left to struggle in futility? In what ways could you describe this enemy's grip as "too mighty for me" (v. 17)? How does God help then?

2. What pictures do verses 13–19 paint in your mind's eye? Describe them.

3. Put yourself in the pictures you just envisioned. What emotions do these pictures evoke?

4. "He rescued me, because He delighted in me" (v. 19), David writes. We usually think of ourselves as "delighting" in God. (See, for example, Psalm 37:4.) But God also takes delight in us! Is that a "Wow!" or a "How?" for you? Explain.

Psalm 18:20–30

This God—His way is perfect;
the word of the LORD proves true;
He is a shield for all those who take refuge in Him.

His Way Is Perfect

I like knowing that I am doing things correctly. Black and white make me secure; gray is scary. Case in point: I began writing this devotion using pen and paper. Why? Well, our computer was down, and after five minutes of instruction from my husband on using a flash drive so I could work at the library and bring it home to his laptop, I decided to go with what I know: pen and paper. I like the familiar—the sure and certain—the stuff of my comfort zone.

I don't think I ever felt more out of my comfort zone than when I first became a mother. There is no feeling quite like that of bringing home a brand-new baby. But scratch the descriptions you find on "new baby" greeting cards and the warm fuzzy setting of baby product television commercials. For me, opening the door of our home with a new baby in my arms and no one but us (why can't you bring home at least one of those wonderful neonatal nurses?!) was absolutely frightening.

The schedule I had sketched out said it was time to eat—but my baby was sleeping. When he woke in the middle of the night crying, wasn't I supposed to be able to tell what kind of a cry it was? Hungry? Uncomfortable? Cold? Hot? Just complaining? To me, the cries began to sound like fingernails on a chalkboard. They added to my anxiety of not knowing what to do while desperately wanting to do it right.

That's right—the vocations I can be certain of are those God has clearly chosen for me. When doubting my worth or direction in life, His perfect wisdom calls me back to where I am today. Knowing this puts my thinking back on track.

As time went on, I became more uncertain. Is one jar of baby food enough? I wanted my baby full but not fat. Full-strength apple juice or half juice, half water? Am I playing with him enough? Maybe I'm overstimulating him. Pacifier or thumb? One nap or two? Does 99.9 degrees count as a fever? Probably the only thing I was certain about was that I had brought the right baby home. Not only did our bracelet numbers match, but he was also by far the only nine-and-a-half-pound, twenty-two-and-a-quarter-inch bundle of joy in that nursery!

Somehow, while navigating my new world of unknowns, I was comforted by knowing that Noah was mine. I knew that it had to be right because God decided, not me, that Noah should be my son. By simply being Noah's mom, I was doing what I was supposed to be doing. I was doing something right after all.

Three babies later, I still had questions as I made daily decisions for each of my four children. It really didn't get any easier. But there was no doubt that each nine-plus-pound bundle belonged to me. God had decided it, so it had to be right!

Now that baby Noah is six-foot-fourteen-year-old-size-11E-shoes Noah, I still have many questions regarding what is best for him—and for Anna, Nathanael, and Luke as well. Not one of them arrived with an instruction manual. Yet, no matter how many

Lisa

mistakes I make (and, boy, do I make them!), my sure calling as their mom remains intact.

Yesterday, we read that God placed us in a broad or spacious place (v. 19). We have a big realm in which to serve Him in our homes, communities, workplaces, and churches. David served God by ruling over Israel. God rescued him from his enemies for that specific purpose. God promised David he would be used to rule the kingdom and to continue the line of the coming Savior. So, when David experienced uncertainty, he still knew that God was working in his life to bring about what He had promised.

Knowing that God has a purpose for our lives gives us a sense of security too. What are some of the vocations, or callings, He has given to you? I am a wife, mother, daughter, sister, niece, and citizen. These callings were given to me by God. I didn't directly seek them out, but rather He directed my life so I could serve in these different vocations.

What exactly is vocation? Simply put, it is loving and serving your neighbor. "And who is my neighbor?" asks the expert in the law (Luke 10:29). As you know, Jesus answers this question with a parable: your neighbor is whoever is lying in your path. We don't have to look too awfully hard to see whom God wants us to serve. He makes it clear. The privilege of serving others is God's gift to us. We serve others because He served us through Jesus' life, death, and resurrection. Jesus, after all, is the ultimate Good Samaritan. Now He chooses to accomplish His perfect purposes through the imperfect hands of people like you and me.

With a family of six, there is always somebody in my path! I don't have to go searching for someone to serve. There is always food to cook, dirt to tackle, arguments to referee, questions to answer, hugs to give, and lost treasures to find. On paper, in the middle of a Bible study book, the importance of the vocation of motherhood is obvious. We all know it is a God-given gift to be a mother and a wife. Who of us wouldn't agree it is a noble task? However, some days, when in the midst of perpetual dishes and laundry, I find myself searching for ways to "pass by on the other side." My God-given vocations no longer feel like gifts from the

Lisa

Creator of the universe. Doubts set in. Maybe serving isn't so noble. I'm tired. Maybe doing something else would make me happier. Maybe I could get some relief and some recognition too! Being acknowledged in the community or appearing indispensable to my congregation is much more appealing than folding a basket of laundry that will be crumpled into the hamper by Friday.

But then I am brought back to the truth of Psalm 18:30: "This God—His way is perfect." That's right—the vocations I can be certain of are those God has clearly chosen for me. When doubting my worth or direction in life, His perfect wisdom calls me back to where I am today. Knowing this puts my thinking back on track. With His help I can leap over a wall (v. 29). He will lighten my darkness (v. 28). He is a shield for me as I take refuge in Him, in His Word and Sacraments (v. 30). "This God is my strong refuge and has made my way blameless" (2 Samuel 22:33).

I still like knowing the right way to do things. I will always shy away from gray areas, although I must admit, that little flash drive does intrigue me! But what will remain black and white for me is that God has blessed me with the vocations He has given me. Someday, my callings may change, but for now I will keep an eye out for all the little opportunities for service that God carefully weaves into my days. I thank Him that He doesn't change, that His promises are intact no matter how I feel, and that He has plans to use me despite my imperfections. His way *is* perfect, and I look forward to serving Him today!

Prayer: Lord, sometimes I am like the Levite and the priest. With my blinders securely fastened, I pass by my neighbor on the other side. Help me to see all of the opportunities You present to me today to serve those You have placed into my life. Thank You that there are no small or insignificant tasks in Your plan. In Jesus' name. *Amen.*

Lisa

wednesday

Personal Study Questions:
Psalm 18:20–30

1. David makes bold claims of righteousness, of blamelessness, in verses 20–24, continuing those claims in verses 25–27 by counting himself among the "merciful" and "blameless." Verse 26 then goes on to say, "With the *purified* You show Yourself pure" (emphasis added).

   a. What clue does this give about the source of the "righteousness," "purity," and "cleanness" David claims for himself?

   b. Do you see yourself—baptized into Christ—as "the blameless," the "righteous," the "purified" one? If so, thank your Lord Jesus for these gifts! If not, ask the Holy Spirit to convince you more fully of the redemption Jesus won for you on Calvary's cross.

2. Note the word pictures in verses 27–30. How many can you find? How does each enlarge your understanding of your Lord's care for you?

3. When have you considered your various vocations and been tempted to doubt the Lord's wisdom in giving you the vocations He has? How could Psalm 18:20 help in times like that?

lisa

Psalm 18:31–42

For who is God, but the LORD? And who is a rock, except our God?—the God who equipped me with strength and made my way blameless. He made my feet like the feet of a deer and set me secure on the heights. He trains my hands for war, so that my arms can bend a bow of bronze. You have given me the shield of Your salvation, and Your right hand supported me, and Your gentleness made me great.

Ready for Battle

We travel a lot. Our favorite vacation spots are Unionville, Michigan, and Ladysmith, Wisconsin. Why? Because those towns are the homes to grandparents! Where else can we go and get all-you-can-eat meals three times a day for a family of six, a comfortable place to sleep, outstanding conversation, lots of fun, and free babysitting?

Over the past seventeen years, we have lived in five different states. Travel times to reach family members'

lisa

66

homes have ranged anywhere from three to seventeen hours. We have traveled with multiple car-seat arrangements and with multiple little ones in diapers. We have gone from vehicles with no air conditioning and no cassette player to a wonderful van with a portable DVD player and front and rear temperature controls. With experiences like this, I like to think we have our travel routine down to a science.

When it's time to pack to go to Grandma's, my kids do a great job. If I give them a list with all of the crucial information (like how many pairs of socks and underwear to bring) they can think through what to put in their duffle bags. The older kids even help the younger ones remember to bring fun stuff to do in the van on the way. As each trip passes and each child gets older, it seems that packing, loading the van—fitting in people, luggage, and dogs—traveling, and unpacking all get just a little easier.

However, I still make a list because there are things we certainly do not want to leave behind. Things like favorite pillows and books, items we have been waiting to show to Grandma and Grandpa, and, for the various toddlers over the years, the all important item that makes everyone's trip more comfortable: BLANKIE!

Yes, if I were to look back at my lists reminding me of last minute things to pack, I believe I would see the word *blankie* written, underlined, and with at least one exclamation point after it on every single list. I don't recall ever forgetting any of those precious, stringy little cloths. And I am sure I would remember a trip when I had!

I credit my mom for my list-making habit. Her favorite advice is "Write it down so you don't forget!" She knows me all too well! My pack-for-traveling lists have their roots in her lists—lists of things to do after school, lists of things to take to school, shopping lists, and to-do lists. Not only are lists helpful for forgetful types such as myself, but they also provide a sense of security and satisfaction as I cross off that final item, knowing that my preparations for wherever I am going or for whatever I am doing are complete.

lisa

God gives us quite a list in our Bible reading for today. It reads as a list of what He does or what He is for us as we travel through each day. It is a list of things that prepare us for our trip out into the world or around our homes each morning. He is our shield. He is our rock. He arms us with strength. He makes our way perfect. He makes our feet like a deer's. He enables us to stand. He trains our hands. He gives us a shield of victory. He broadens our path. We are certainly well-equipped each day!

Remember that as God's baptized child, you are forgiven! You are already under His care and protection, whether or not you remember it. The list of things He does for us in no way depends upon the list of things we do. As our God strengthens us and equips us through His Word and His Sacraments, we are ready for anything!

David experienced these very things as God saved him from his enemies. God provided the perfect protection, strength, and ability that brought David safely and triumphantly through much trouble.

As we read David's words, it sounds as though he is comfortable and confident in this armor of God. It is exactly what David needs. It is exactly what we need. It is not like the armor of Saul (1 Samuel 17:38–39)—ill-fitting and cumbersome—but sometimes we act as if it is. We often don't want to take time to be properly equipped for our daily battles. We wake up and follow our routine, too often ignoring the list of things that would add to the strength God already provides for us.

What's on that list? Reading God's Word. Praying. Attending the Divine Service. Receiving the Lord's Supper. Participating in Bible class. Doing family devotions. We might decide that it feels cumbersome to squeeze such things into our day, our week, our comfortable routine. We have our own list of things that seem immovable—our must dos—and preparing for battle just doesn't fit nicely into our plan, so these nourishing activities too easily get tabled or ignored.

Finish this sentence: "I wouldn't be caught dead leaving the house without _____." A typical answer might be putting on mascara or lipstick, brushing my teeth, or curling my hair. If you have children, try this one: "I would never let them out the door in the morning without_____." What fits here? Lunch money? Backpack? Cell phone? Which thing, if forgotten,

68

is important enough that you make a trip to school to take it to them?

What on our lists get the underscores and exclamation marks? What are our favorite security blankets? What do we absolutely need to get through the day?

We are all guilty of failing to nourish ourselves with the things God provides. We fail to take advantage of the benefits that come from reading His Word daily, praying, and joyfully attending worship. We, as daughters of God, desire to have at the top of our lists the things He tells us are good for our daily walk with Him. But, in our sinful flesh, we fail. Added to our list now is "feeling the burden of failure . . . again."

Take a minute to get a piece of paper, a sticky note, or whatever you like to use for your daily lists. As my mom would say, "Write it down so you don't forget!" List the things you know God will do for you today. Put "His way is perfect" (v. 30) or "He is a shield" (v. 30). Add "Your right hand supported me" (v. 35) and "You equipped me with strength for the battle" (v. 39). Give it a couple of underlines and an exclamation point for good measure.

Remember that as God's baptized child, you are forgiven! You are already under His care and protection whether or not you remember it. The list of things He does for us in no way depends upon the list of things we do. As our God strengthens us and equips us through His Word and His Sacraments, we are ready for anything! God's children are at the top of His list. Underlined, surrounded by exclamation points, forgiven, never forgotten, and ready for battle. The God who redeemed David redeemed you, calls you His own, and sustains you. He has made you ready for whatever is on your list today.

Lisa

Prayer: Father, thank You that Your list of promises to me is unchanging. Increase in me a desire to read Your Word and to be reminded of the forgiveness and strength You give to me. Thank You for graciously equipping me for my daily battles. Thank You for claiming victory for me in Christ Jesus. In His name. **Amen.**

Lisa

thursday

Personal Study Questions:
Psalm 18:31–42

1. In these verses, David uses a second extended metaphor, comparing God's care to the kind of help that would save a warrior's life in battle. Just as a very real thunderstorm likely helped frame the words of verses 7–19, so, too, memory of several very real battles may have come to David's mind as he penned verses 31–42. Think, for example, about David's very first battle—the one he fought with the giant Goliath.

   What words or phrases from verses 31–42 could describe the victory God won for His people through David that day (1 Samuel 17)?

2. While the kind of warfare the psalmist describes is not, as our mothers might have said, very ladylike, as God's daughters we find ourselves at war, spiritually speaking, as often as do God's sons.

   a. What spiritual battle(s) are especially fierce for you today?

   b. Which descriptions of God's help from the list in verses 31–42 bring you special comfort as you consider your struggle?

lisa

Psalm 18:43–50

For this I will praise You, O LORD, among the nations, and sing to Your name. Great salvation He brings to His king, and shows steadfast love to His anointed, to David and his offspring forever.

Valued Forever

I have a history of losing things. Important things. Things of great value. To date, I have lost my Baptism locket, an achievement-award wristwatch, my high school class ring, and the diamond out of my engagement ring. I have also lost a lot of things that weren't so important. I can't even tell you what they were. Why were some of these possessions important and some not? I guess it depends upon the value I chose to place on them.

One thing I lost that has more value to me than any of the items listed above is a drawing my husband made when he was five or six. It was a picture of an airplane, drawn with red crayon, with his name in little-boy print

Lisa

across the bottom. His mom gladly let me have it, so I brought it home, planning to frame it and hang it in my boys' room. But I can't find it anywhere. I know I carefully put it in the proverbial "very special place" . . . and I hope to someday remember just where that is. (Yes, Mom, I should have written it down!) I was able to replace my diamond, but that drawing is a one-of-a-kind.

Why do we value what we do? What makes us decide that one particular thing is more important than another?

At my house, milk rings have great value. Milk rings? Yup. You know—the plastic rings that are left around the neck of a milk jug after you twist off the cap? Not the ones that come off in a broken strip; those don't count. I'm talking about the ones that remain a complete circle.

How much are they worth, you ask? Well, that depends upon their color. Blue 2-percent rings are plentiful—only 1 point each. A green ring is worth 5, a red ring 100, and a purple ring 500. But a coveted and very rare gold ring from our favorite brand of malted milk? Two thousand points! Who knows how these values were determined, but my boys decided that this is so, and now there are plastic containers and covered boxes filled with a colorful assortment of plastic rings in safe keeping upstairs in my house. I won't reveal their exact location—just in case.

My kids also value the hymnal that sits on our piano because it was Great-Grandpa Balko's. They value the dented metal saucepan that hangs above the kitchen sink because great-grandma used it every morning to make her oatmeal.

Have you ever watched *Antiques Roadshow*? I think that some of the prices they put on different old items are unbelievable. It always intrigues me that a small clay pot can be worth thousands of dollars while a beautiful tapestry or painting will bring only a few hundred dollars. What determines the value of these small clay pots? Why are they worth so much?

I think that either we are taught or we choose what to value. If we hear someone we respect singing the praises of a particular object, we value it more. It would take some pretty hefty persuading to get Luke, my five-year-old, to give up his gold milk ring.

Lisa

Friday

Personal Study Questions: Psalm 18:43–50

1. In verse 46, David notes, "The LORD lives!" Old Testament writers frequently used the title "the living God" to denote that Yahweh is the God who acts on behalf of His people. The holy writers contrast the living God with the dead, dumb idols of the heathen who cannot respond to their worshipers' needs. See, for example, Deuteronomy 5:26; 1 Samuel 17:26; and Isaiah 37:17.

   a. How does David know that the living God values him? How do you?

   b. What has the living God done for David, according to verses 43–50?

   c. What is David's response in verses 49–50?

2. When has the Lord shown Himself to be the living God in your own life during the past few days? What is *your* response?

Group Bible Study for Week Two
Psalm 18

1. In what ways does Psalm 18 fit in this collection of psalms, all of which tell God's "wonderful deeds"?

2. Talk with members of your group about the personal pronouns in verses 1–3. Why do you suppose David uses such personal language throughout this psalm? What does the Holy Spirit intend to communicate by it?

3. Consider the description of God in the last phrase of verse 7: "because He was angry."

   a. What has stirred up God's anger at this point in the psalm?

   b. How would you describe the Lord's actions in response to His anger?

   c. Which adjectives best describe your experience in knowing that your Lord responds to your cries for help with the same intense, fierce love described here?

4. In verse 30, David asserts, "The word of the LORD proves true." Why, then, do we so often struggle to find time to read the Word and use the courage it takes to act on that Word?

5. Jesus' gentleness truly has "made [us] great" (v. 35). How has it done that?

6. What additional words and phrases from the psalm particularly caught your eye this week and encouraged your heart? Read them to the group, and explain why you chose them.

7. Which faith narrative from the past week helped explain or accent the truths of Psalm 18 in a particularly powerful way for you? Explain as specifically as you can.

8. With all this in mind, for what would the group like to praise your Savior-God in today's closing prayer? For what will you ask Him?

Week Three

Psalm 30

¹ I will extol You, O Lord, for You have drawn me up
and have not let my foes rejoice over me.

² O Lord my God, I cried to You for help,
and You have healed me.

³ O Lord, You have brought up my soul from Sheol;
You restored me to life from among those who go down to
the pit.

⁴ Sing praises to the Lord, O you His saints,
and give thanks to His holy name.

⁵ For His anger is but for a moment,
and His favor is for a lifetime.
Weeping may tarry for the night,
but joy comes with the morning.

⁶ As for me, I said in my prosperity,
"I shall never be moved."

^{7} By Your favor, O LORD,
You made my mountain stand strong;
You hid Your face;
I was dismayed.

^{8} To You, O LORD, I cry,
and to the Lord I plead for mercy:

^{9} "What profit is there in my death,
if I go down to the pit?
Will the dust praise You?
Will it tell of Your faithfulness?

^{10} Hear, O LORD, and be merciful to me!
O LORD, be my helper!"

^{11} You have turned for me my mourning into dancing;
You have loosed my sackcloth
and clothed me with gladness,

^{12} that my glory may sing Your praise and not be silent.
O LORD my God, I will give thanks to You forever!

Lisa Hellyer

Psalm 30:1–3

I will extol You, O LORD, for You have drawn me up and have not let my foes rejoice over me. O LORD my God, I cried to You for help, and You have healed me. O LORD, You have brought up my soul from Sheol; You restored me to life from among those who go down to the pit.

Rescued from the Pit

ne beautiful spring afternoon, I was enjoying hanging out with my sister and her soon-to-be husband. Since it was such a glorious day, we decided to go for a walk at a nearby lake. The lake was nestled in a valley below, surrounded by nothing but a green, tree-lined hillside.

Getting down to the lake was no problem at all—we followed a paved pathway. However, getting up the hill from the lake was a different story. Despite my best efforts to convince them, my sister and her fiancé didn't see the beauty in being adventurous. "Why take the sidewalk," I said, "when you can have more fun taking the shortcut."

I was young, invincible, and adventurous—the steep hillside was definitely the best option for me. I started out just fine and even thought how fun it was going to be to stand waiting for them at the top.

But somewhere in the middle of my energetic ascent, getting traction on the wet and extremely muddy hillside suddenly became difficult. It hadn't looked muddy from my perspective at the bottom; it had looked only fun and easy. However, before I knew it, my sister and future brother-in-law were standing at the top of the hill and enjoying quite a laugh at the sight of me. I had slipped a few times and now had mud on my shoes and clothing. They urged me to go back down the hill and take the long way up, the paved way. But I wasn't about to admit defeat. Eventually, my sister's fiancé made his way to me—down into the muddy ravine—and he encouraged me, laughed with me, and gave me occasional boosts and footholds to get me all the way to the top.

The psalmist says, "I will extol You, O Lord, for You have drawn me up" (v. 1). There are times in life when we are in a pit. Sometimes we're there because we've decided to do things our own way. We've lost sight of the fact that Jesus knows us, loves us, and wants what is best for us. We've ceased paying attention to the guidance and direction of the Holy Spirit speaking to us in God's Word. We have decided that we know better than anyone what is best for us. We have chosen to believe the lies of Satan rather than trust in the promises of God. At that point, it is just a matter of time until we see that we're in a pit, wondering how we got into such a mess. Ideally, it doesn't take long for our hearts to understand that our sin dragged us down there. And we have no one else to blame but ourselves.

On the other hand, sometimes we're in a pit because of some-

lisa

one else's decisions. When those we love make poor choices, it is easy to get caught up in and suffer the consequences of their sin. We didn't do anything wrong. We didn't make the bad decision. Nonetheless, we're in the pit just the same. My future brother-in-law had made it out of the ravine just fine, without one spot of dirt on him, but because of my stubbornness, he ended up with mud on him as well.

God doesn't expect us to do something extravagant or extraordinary for Him—those are His specialties. He simply enables us to live in response to all He does for us. So whether we are taking kids to soccer practice or piano lessons, whether we are cleaning house or making dinner, whether we are volunteering at church or working elsewhere, we do it all with gratitude in our hearts for our rescuer, Jesus.

Sometimes we're in a pit just because we live in a sinful and broken world. Jesus reminds us in John 16:33, "In the world you will have tribulation." That's it. He doesn't mince words, He doesn't sugar coat it, and He doesn't try to disguise it in any way. Jesus says it just the way it is. He tells us to expect hardship. It's not a matter of "if"—it's a matter of "when." Trouble will come through relationship struggles, the loss of loved ones, financial problems, the loss of a job, illness, or tragedy in our own lives or in the lives of complete strangers. And when those difficult days are upon us, we find ourselves in a pit of despair, loneliness, anger, bitterness, or depression.

What matters least is how we got in the pit—as the result of our own decisions, the actions of others, or just the circumstances of living in a sinful world. What matters most is who gets us out.

I was overjoyed to be out of that muddy pit. But even more, I was grateful to my sister's fiancé for his willingness to come in after me and for sticking with me until I was in the clear. That's what happens in our lives too. God has rescued us through our Savior, Jesus Christ, who got us out of the mess of our sin. How can we help but praise our rescuer?

It's interesting to note that the psalmist doesn't spend any time describing the pit or even what got him there but instead focuses on our gracious heavenly Father. He says, "O LORD my God, I cried to You for help, and You have healed me. O LORD, You have brought up my soul from Sheol; You restored me to life from among those who go down to the pit" (v. 2). That's a response of praise, of sheer gratitude.

We are helpless and hopeless without a Savior, without a rescuer, without someone willing to get muddy on our behalf. Jesus did that for us. When the Son of God left the glory of heaven and came to earth to take on our human flesh, He came to us in the pit of our broken, sin-filled lives. He came to rescue us. There is no way we can save ourselves. Despite my best attempts, I wasn't getting out of that ravine that day. I tried, but to no avail. Someone had to be willing to climb in with me to help me out. On the cross, Jesus was willing to take our sins upon Himself. Because of Jesus, who is now resurrected from the dead, you and I are fully forgiven; we enjoy a restored relationship with God, our heavenly Father.

How do we respond? We respond by offering our lives as a sacrifice of praise to the Lord! We give our everyday, ordinary lives to Him as a living sacrifice (Romans 12:1). That's it! God doesn't expect us to do something extravagant or extraordinary for Him—those are His specialties. He simply enables us to live in response to all He does for us. So whether we are taking kids to soccer practice or piano lessons, whether we are cleaning house or making dinner, whether we are volunteering at church or working elsewhere, we do it all with gratitude in our hearts for our rescuer, Jesus.

Since that hike to the lake many years ago, my sister, brother-in-law, and I have enjoyed a good laugh about it. What I find interesting is that not once have they reminded me that I was stubborn, that I chose the wrong way, that I made their car a muddy mess, or that I dragged another person into the mud with me. My downfalls have not been the focus of the story. That isn't to say that my downfalls aren't obvious, in fact anyone who hears the story knows all too well what led to that mess, but it isn't held against me. Praise be to God, who sees us in our pits, comes to us right where we are, and rescues us by lifting us out. He has healed us, restored our lives, and drawn us up through faith in His Son.

lisa

Prayer: Dear heavenly Father, thank You for Your faithfulness. Thank You for Your Son's willingness to climb into the messiness of our lives and to rescue us by His death and resurrection. Enable us by Your Holy Spirit to offer our everyday, ordinary lives to You in gratitude as a sacrifice of praise. In Jesus' name. **Amen.**

Lisa

monday

Personal Study Questions:
Psalm 30:1–3

1. How does the muddy hill scene and rescue that opens today's faith narrative help you more deeply appreciate the psalmist's words in verses 1–3?

2. Psalm 30 begins with a series of "you haves" and one "you have not."

   a. List these from verses 1–3.

   b. For which of these same blessings can you join David in extolling the Lord?

3. The reformer Martin Luther defines what he calls the "high spiritual afflictions of the devil, which are sadness, depression, terror, despair, doubt, the perils of death, and similar poisonous, fiery darts" (from *Reading the Psalms with Luther*, p. 72). Consider the psalms you have already studied in depth in this volume (Psalms 9 and 18) and the first three verses of Psalm 30.

   a. Which of these "darts" has David experienced? Which have you?

   b. What have you learned from these psalms about the best ways to defend yourself from these darts?

lisa

Psalm 30:4–5

Sing praises to the Lord, O you His saints, and give thanks to His holy name. For His anger is but for a moment, and His favor is for a lifetime. Weeping may tarry for the night, but joy comes with the morning.

Joy Comes with the Morning

Among my fondest memories are those of my grandpa. I remember loving him, spending time with him, and talking to him. One of the things I loved talking to my grandpa about was life in the church. He was not only my grandpa, he was also my pastor, and I would ask question after question about all kinds of things regarding church life and things I was learning in Sunday School. I shared with him my secret hope of one day being a church worker. He would smile and encourage me to do whatever

God called me to do. Sometimes when we talked, I would sit at his feet while he played with my hair. He would rub my hair and tuck it behind my ear. And when he was done, I would put my hair back in place so he could tuck it behind my ear all over again. I absolutely adored him, which is why I didn't like disappointing him.

At some point in my later elementary school years, I got into big trouble. What I did isn't important, but I will tell you that it involved firemen and fire trucks. I was in some hot water, and I knew it! The minute I walked in the door, my mom knew immediately that I was guilty of something. When she heard fire engines and sirens, her instincts were confirmed, but as a single mom, she knew she would need some help with this one. So I was surprised when all she said was "Go to your room." What a relief! I had unintentionally and accidentally started the woods on fire and all I got was "Go to your room"? This was my lucky day! I figured I would get the usual punishment—no TV for a week, no playing outside for a week, and I would have to go to bed early for a week. Not too bad. But still, as I sat in my room, I had a nagging thought that this deed was worse than other things I'd done that required punishment.

What I wasn't prepared for was the quiet knock on my door. I decided it was best to ignore it and hope against hope that whoever was knocking would go away. That didn't work. The person who knocked came in uninvited, sat on the edge of my bed, and quietly said my name. How could she do this to me? Why not spank me? Why not ground me for a month? two months? a year? In her turmoil over how to punish me, my mom had called my grandpa. I was horrified. I didn't want him to know what I had done, and I certainly didn't want to endure his anger and his disappointment. While I don't remember my punishment or what he said to me, I do remember the quiet tears that fell from my grandpa's face that day, and I remember feeling like I wanted to hide forever and never have to look him in the eyes again. It seemed at the time that his anger and disappointment would last forever, but then came the embrace and the softly spoken words, "I love you." How

lisa

could that be? I was disobedient and didn't deserve my grandpa's love or forgiveness. It helps me understand more deeply the words of the psalmist: "For His anger is but for a moment, and His favor is for a lifetime. Weeping may tarry for the night, but joy comes with the morning" (v. 5).

When life seems hopeless, joy comes with the morning. When your boss is overly demanding, joy comes with the morning. When a good friend betrays your trust, joy comes with the morning. When your child disappoints you, joy comes with the morning. When you're living with the consequences of your own sin, joy comes with the morning.

No matter what we are enduring—consequences of sin, pain from a broken relationship, struggles with work or family issues, or discipline from our heavenly Father, we can rest in the assurance that it is momentary—it won't last forever. What's difficult is that in the midst of it all, we sometimes lose sight of God's promises in His Word. Sometimes it feels like the pain will never go away or that the brokenness won't heal or that our struggles won't end. Jeremiah reminds us in Lamentations 3:21–24, "But this I call to mind, and therefore I have hope: The steadfast love of the LORD never ceases; His mercies never come to an end; they are new every morning; great is Your faithfulness. 'The LORD is my portion,' says my soul, 'therefore I will hope in Him.'" Jeremiah reminds himself that although the struggle seems eternal, it isn't. God is faithful. His love and compassion are new to us each day. Despite the struggle, joy always comes in the morning!

Think about what Mary, Jesus' mother, His relatives, friends, and disciples must have been going through the day Jesus was crucified. The pain of watching Him beaten, nailed to a cross, and taking His last breath must have been unbearable. They were filled with sorrow. Perhaps they recounted their time with Jesus and wondered what had happened for it all to end in His horrible suffering and death. The women who made their way to the tomb that Sunday morning had probably been up most of the night, weeping. In fact, when Mary Magdalene reached the tomb, she was still crying. When she realized Jesus was not there, that He had risen from the grave, we can only imagine her joy. She was so happy to see Jesus, she ran to Him, embraced Him, and then did exactly what Jesus told her

to do. She went to the disciples with the good news: "I have seen the Lord!" (John 20:18). Joy comes with the morning!

When life seems hopeless, joy comes with the morning. When your boss is overly demanding, joy comes with the morning. When a good friend betrays your trust, joy comes with the morning. When your child disappoints you, joy comes with the morning. When you're living with the consequences of your own sin, joy comes with the morning. God is faithful. He loves us, knows us, and wants what is best for us. At times, the best thing for us is to experience the consequences and pain of disobedience in order to come out on the other side molded and shaped to be more like Jesus.

Jesus was faithful, trustworthy, and "obedient to the point of death, even death on a cross" (Philippians 2:8). Because He endured God's wrath against our sin for us, we can endure the hardships that come our way. We can understand why the psalmist would tell us to "Sing praises to the LORD, O you His saints, and give thanks to His holy name" (v. 4). To someone who doesn't have a relationship with Jesus, these words must seem like nonsense. Why would we praise the Lord in the midst of turmoil, pain, and struggle? We praise and we sing because we trust the One who endured His cross, experienced death and hell on our behalf, and came out victorious in the morning. Because Jesus brought joy in the morning that first Easter, He assures those who know Him as Savior and Lord that joy comes with the morning for us as well.

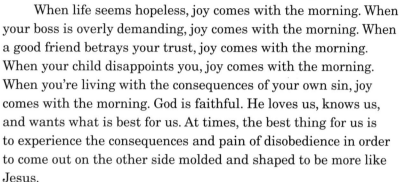

Prayer: Lord Jesus Christ, in my darkest moments, when life is hard and pain is real, help me to cling to Your Word that joy comes with the morning. Help me to praise You no matter the difficulty of my circumstances and to recall Your compassion and love that are renewed to me each and every day. I praise You, O Lord. Amen.

Lisa

tuesday

Personal Study Questions:
Psalm 30:4–5

1. Why would we "give thanks to *His holy name*" (v. 5, emphasis added); in other words, why doesn't the text simply enjoin us to "give thanks to *Him*"?

2. What two contrasts do you note in verse 5?

3. Compare Isaiah 54:9 with Psalm 30:5.

   a. What makes our Lord's promised favor, His commitment to dismiss His anger at our sin, so wonderful?

   b. How does the story of sin and pardon in today's faith narrative illustrate our Savior-God's compassion toward us, His children?

Psalm 30:6–7

As for me, I said in my prosperity, "I shall never be moved." By Your favor, O LORD, You made my mountain stand strong; You hid Your face; I was dismayed.

On Christ, the Solid Rock, I Stand

As a youth minister, on several occasions I've enjoyed taking students snow skiing. I grew up in south Florida, where I didn't have much opportunity to learn the ins and outs of this sport. However, after moving to the Midwest, I learned quickly how to hold my own on the slopes. By "hold my own," I mean I can strap on a pair of skis, make my way to the easy or intermediate slopes, and not kill myself or anyone else in the process. I've mastered the skill of using the chairlift, and I can stay upright from the top of the hill all the way to the bottom. In the end, that's all that matters in skiing.

On some of these trips, I got crazy and joined the kids in a game of follow the leader. I usually ended up crashing and burning, but it wasn't overly embarrassing. One year, I believed I was finally getting the hang of it and even seriously contemplated joining the kids on some of the black diamond (expert) hills. But I decided that a few more practice runs down the intermediates would be a good idea. I was better than good—a few more years and the Olympic team might call me in! Okay, I really wasn't good at all.

On this day, I was having a great time cruising down a mountain when I heard an out-of-control skier behind me. Just as I turned my head to see where the noise was coming from, the person making all the racket hit me. I think she was saying, "Watch out, I can't stop!" The next thing I knew, I was careening out of control, fighting with all I had to keep from falling. In my attempt to stay upright, I had gotten myself turned around and was now going down the mountain backward! I quickly assessed that this was not good. I worked very hard to turn myself around and by some miracle, I accomplished this task. I checked my surroundings. Both skies were still on my feet, each hand still held a pole, I wasn't hurt, and I was still going down the hill. Amazing! I was so excited I boasted to the teens from my church who were watching the whole thing. Raising my arms in the air, I proclaimed, "I am so good! Did you see that?" Just as I began to enjoy my victory and started feeling secure in my skiing abilities, something unexpected happened. I'm not even sure what it was. I don't know if I hit something or something hit me. What I do know is that I was laid out flat on the side of the hill, surrounded by a bunch of laughing teenagers. How quickly my sense of security vanished!

Even if everything around us—family, friends, job, and so on—is washed away, we still have our foundation. We still have Jesus, our only hope, our only security. After all, it was Jesus who left the security of heaven for the insecurity of our world—a world that despised and rejected Him. Thanks be to God that He understood our plight of insecurity that comes with sin and that He had a plan to save us and to offer us eternal life.

Lisa

Could that be what David was talking about in this psalm when he said, "As for me, I said in my prosperity, 'I shall never be moved.' By Your favor, O Lᴏʀᴅ, You made my mountain stand strong" (v. 7)? When I was enjoying the slopes, I certainly felt as if I could never be shaken—but I was wrong!

In a world full of insecurities, I don't know how we can feel secure about anything. Like David, we buy into and become comfortable with a false sense of security. We think that if we have enough money in the bank, everything will be fine. Or we convince ourselves that our careers, families, relationships, abilities, or health will give us the security we need. We take comfort in our homes and cars and material possessions with which we surround ourselves. Are we so foolish as to think these things are guaranteed in our future? Are we so foolish as to think that we are indispensable and therefore irreplaceable? Indeed, sometimes we are that foolish! We resonate with David's sentiment, "I will never be moved." Intellectually we know that life is full of uncertainties. But what we know in our head and what we live out on a daily basis don't always match up. We're like the man who built his house on sand: "And the rain fell, and the floods came, and the winds blew and beat against that house, and it fell, and great was the fall of it" (Matthew 7:27). The storms of life have a way of giving us a beating. And these beatings seem more harsh to those who have no hope in Christ, those whose foundation is not built on Christ alone.

A friend of mine received word that she had colon cancer. Did that news shake her a little? Absolutely. But it didn't change her foundation. She wasn't trusting in her health, she had her trust in the God who gave her that health. She faced the chemo, the sickness, the day-to-day struggles, and the frequent checkups with a joy and a peace that the world around her didn't understand. She was a witness to the fact that Jesus was her security and that she trusted Him for everything, including her health and her very life.

The question isn't *will* a storm come but *what* storm will come. Some of us already have or will face the storm of divorce, a sick child, rebellious children, loss of a job, a spouse addicted to pornography, failing health of a parent, infertility, the tragic death of a loved one, and so on. Storms rage all around us, and if our security is founded in anything but the Savior who either calms the storm or calms us, then we're headed for trouble. David reminds us in this psalm of what it was like to have God hide His face—"You hid Your face; I was dismayed" (v. 7). It's not a good place to be. Without Jesus walking through life's storms with us, our days are much more difficult and even, perhaps, unbearable. Wouldn't you rather join in the hymn, "His oath, His covenant and blood Support me in the raging flood; When ev'ry earthly prop gives way, He then is all my hope and stay. On Christ, the solid rock, I stand; All other ground is sinking sand, All other ground is sinking sand"? (*LSB* 576:3).

Even if everything around us—family, friends, job, and so on—is washed away, we still have our foundation. We still have Jesus, our only hope, our only security. After all, it was Jesus who left the security of heaven for the insecurity of our world—a world that despised and rejected Him. Thanks be to God that He understood our plight that comes with sin and that He had a plan to save us and to offer us eternal life. When we face life's uncertainties, we can be secure in the knowledge that our sins are paid for and that the blood Jesus shed on the cross has redeemed us.

Prayer: Father, forgive us when we look to all kinds of things and people for a sense of security. Help us to trust wholly in You for our day-to-day security and for our eternal home with You. In Jesus' name. **Amen.**

wednesday

Personal Study Questions:
Psalm 30:6–7

1. Verses 6–7 contain another contrast.

   a. How would you define it?

   b. What makes the ski story from today's faith narrative an apt illustration of this contrast?

   c. When have you similarly fallen for Satan's temptation to self-reliance and spiritual pride?

   d. How did your Savior draw you back to Himself and to reliance on Him? What part of that process seemed as though He had "hidden His face"?

2. How do we know that our God never disciplines us in anger, only in love?

lisa

Psalm 30:8–10

To You, O LORD, I cry, and to the LORD I plead for mercy:
"What profit is there in my death, if I go down to the pit?
Will the dust praise You? Will it tell of Your faithfulness? Hear,
O LORD, and be merciful to me! O LORD, be my helper!"

God, our Helper

When I was in college, two of my grandparents died, and I developed an unhealthy fear of death. I thought about dying quite a bit and worried how and when it would happen. I made deals with the Lord about how I wanted to die. I didn't want to die yet—I simply wasn't ready. I had too much living to do, and I love life! Somehow, I made my way through the fear of thinking about death. However, it wasn't until I had a near-death experience that I was able to face that fear head-on.

Lisa

This happened on a canoe retreat with some high school students. Most of the creek we were canoeing was knee-deep, but a few places were well over my head. At one point we saw signs warning us about a dangerous undertow ahead. Teens don't pay much attention to things like that. As we approached the area the signs warned us about, one of the high school students started guiding my canoe toward the rock where the undertow was located. Despite my best attempts to discourage him, my canoe, my canoe partner, and I were quickly sucked against the rock face. I couldn't believe how strong the current was. I was helpless getting the canoe free. With every attempt, we were only sucked further under the cave wall where water was flowing. Soon the water took the canoe and me under. Unfortunately, I was not wearing a life jacket, and my legs stretched out in front of me under a thwart, a bar that goes across the canoe. I was trapped inside the canoe that was now upside down in the water. As I struggled to get out and find the surface, I had two thoughts: "I'm going to die, but I'm okay with that," and "How will the adult volunteers handle this with the high school students?" When I came face to face with the fact that I was going to die, I was surprised to discover that I had total peace. I was ready to go to heaven whenever the Lord called me. I knew that whatever happened I would be fine, but knowing that didn't stop me from thinking about the people I would leave behind. I wanted to be there for them. I wanted to continue to be their youth minister. I wanted to be the one to comfort them and pray with them and watch them grow in their faith.

Another thing I've processed about this experience is this: although I was at peace at the thought of dying, it didn't stop me from fighting for life and calling out to the Lord for help. I was ready, but I didn't want to die quite yet. I wanted to live, and I asked God to let me. God did help me. I somehow got out of the canoe, found the rock face, and came to the surface, where I took a very deep breath of air.

Looking at today's psalm, I have no doubt that David was ready to die, but like me I wonder if he didn't want to leave this life at that particular time. He wrote, "What profit is there in my

Lisa

death, if I go down to the pit? Will the dust praise You? Will it tell of Your faithfulness?" (v. 9). David knew he would praise his King on either side of life, but he also knew that once his life was gone from this world, there would be one less voice on earth praising God and one less person alive telling of God's faithfulness.

As long as we're on this side of heaven, we rely on God's strength to see us through. Like David, we come to the realization that we can do nothing on our own. Therefore we join our cries with his, "Hear, O LORD, and be merciful to me! O LORD, be my helper!" (v. 10).

I totally understand what David is saying because I love this life, but at the same time I realize that this world is not my home. There are days when I feel like a foreigner, and I long to be free from it all. Like on those days when the morals of our society seem to have reached an all-time low. When the news of violence reaches my ears and I wonder if it can get any worse. When tragedy strikes those I love and the pain seems almost unbearable. On those days, I wonder how long it will be until the Lord returns and takes us all home. I find myself anxious for that day.

But those aren't the only days that have me longing for my heavenly home. Sometimes life is just difficult. Are there days when you long to see Jesus face to face? Are there days when you could join the woman in the old Calgon commercial pleading, "Take me away"? On those days, nobody seems to appreciate all you do to keep the family functioning, and the stress from work is too much. On those days, financial troubles seem to chase you—the car tires need to be replaced, the doctor bills were higher than expected, and the property taxes are due. On those days, everyone needs a piece of you, and there isn't much more you can give. On those days, life can seem overwhelming, and your soul desires to be free of a sin-filled and broken world.

As long as we are on this side of heaven, we rely on God's strength to see us through. Like David, we realize that we can do nothing on our own. That is when we join our cries with his: "Hear, O LORD, and be merciful to me! O LORD, be my helper!" (v. 10). There is no doubt that we will struggle in this life. Jesus tells us, "In the world you will have tribulation" (John 16:33). That isn't

lisa

exactly the kind of promise we want to hear. And if that were the end of the promise, we would be in a real mess. But Jesus continues, "But take heart; I have overcome the world." That's not just good news, it's great news! In His life on earth, Jesus experienced trouble too. And I'm sure there were days when He longed to be back in the glories of heaven. In fact, just after the transfiguration, the disciples were having some trouble healing a demon-possessed boy. Jesus said to them, "O faithless and twisted generation, how long am I to be with you? How long am I to bear with you?" (Matthew 17:17).

But bear with us is what He did—and then some. He went all the way to the cross of Calvary on our behalf. He didn't just put up with us; He died for us. And not only that, but He rose again and ascended into heaven to prepare a place for us. One day, our voices will no longer sing praises from this earth, but instead we will be standing before the very throne of God, joining with the voices of angels and the faithful who have gone before us. With perfect resurrected bodies and standing with our crucified and resurrected Lord, we will enjoy a new heaven and a new earth that knows nothing of death (Revelation 21:4). No longer will we be crying to the Lord for help, for we will be home with Him forever. Until that day, we cry out to Him. Whether in life or in death, God is our helper.

Prayer: Heavenly Father, thank You for the life You've given me here on earth and for the opportunity to praise You and to proclaim Your faithfulness. Thank You for the promise of eternity, where I will praise You forever. In Jesus' name. **Amen.**

Lisa

thursday

Personal Study Questions:
Psalm 30:8–10

1. These verses evidently summarize the prayer David prayed after his fall into pride and the subsequent dismay he experienced when God "hid [His] face" (v. 7).

   a. What makes this prayer fitting and appropriate for that situation?

   b. In what ways might we consider it a near-death experience?

   c. How do these words offer for our use a prayer we could also pray—not once, but perpetually throughout our lives here on earth?

2. How does verse 9 tie worship and witness to a realization of the Lord's mercy?

Psalm 30:11–12

You have turned for me my mourning into dancing; You have loosed my sackcloth and clothed me with gladness, that my glory may sing Your praise and not be silent. O LORD my God, I will give thanks to You forever!

God Is Faithful

I have taken many road trips with teenagers. Most of these outings have been incredible, but there is one I never want to forget. This was a weekend adventure with a group of high school students that required several vehicles and a six-hour journey.

Everything was going great—we left on time, we enjoyed a pleasant dinner break during the trip, and everyone was in a good mood. Following the lead vehicle, I kept my eyes on the church van behind me. At some point, the driver of the church van decided I wasn't going fast enough, so he pulled into the left lane to pass me. As he passed, I waved to the passengers only to notice it wasn't our van. How long had I been watching the wrong vehicle?! (This took place before the age of cell phones, so I wasn't sure what to do.) To try to make sure we were all together, I passed the lead vehicle then pulled onto the shoulder. But the other church van was nowhere in sight! We waited and waited, but still no sign of the van or, more important, the treasures that van was transporting!

One of our teens noticed that I was anxious and suggested that we gather everyone for prayer. *Why didn't I think of that!*

You and I have been delivered. We have been and continue to be the recipients of God's faithfulness and goodness. God was faithful to His promise to deliver us from the greatest bondage we have ever known—the bondage of sin, death, and the power of the devil.

Chad, a student leader, prayed that God would help us find our missing friends and that they would be safe. After the prayer, we decided one van would drive ahead, and we in our van would search for the "needle in a haystack." I drove while the kids did the looking. We searched every exit. I was worried that something terrible had happened or that the trip would have to be canceled. After forty-five minutes or so of searching, I told the students we would search one more exit before deciding our next plan of action. Before we took the exit, the teens thought we should pray again. Our prayer was the same—God, help us find them and let them be safe. The kids kept their eyes open during the prayer just to be sure they didn't miss anything. Just as I was taking the exit, one of the students proclaimed in a voice that scared me half to death, "There they are!" The excitement inside our van was unbelievable. We'd found the needle in the haystack, and they were all fine. They had experienced a blowout on the highway and waited for help to come. They had prayed that we would notice they weren't with us anymore and would find them. The reunion was sweet! The kids were excited to see one another and busy telling one another about their adventures while apart. It wasn't long before someone remembered that we should thank God for all He had done.

This experience was a miracle, a testimony of God's faithfulness. It was a "Yes" from God in answer to our prayers. It was an

Lisa

104

example of what the psalmist spoke of when he said, "You have turned for me my mourning into dancing; You have loosed my sackcloth and clothed me with gladness" (v. 11). I don't think anyone in our group was wailing, and I'm quite certain no one had broken out the sackcloth. However, all of us felt worry, fear, confusion, and uncertainty. In the midst of it all was Jesus, who heard our cries for help, knew about the fear in our hearts, and understood the depth of our worry.

My friend, God is faithful! He knows us, and He knows all about the fear, worry, confusion, and uncertainties in our lives. He knows what keeps us tossing and turning through the night. He knows the first prayer on our lips in the morning. He knows the depth of our pain and the extent of our brokenness. He knows the heaviness of our burdens. He knows, and He is faithful! But God's faithfulness doesn't mean He is going to snap His fingers and fix everything right now. God sees what we can't see. He sees the whole picture, whereas we see our world only from our vantage point. God has perfect timing, whereas we have a tendency to want Him to work according to our schedule. We live in a world of instant gratification, and we sometimes think even that takes too long. However, when we cry out to God for deliverance, we can trust Him wholeheartedly and wait for His timing.

So what does God's faithfulness mean? It means that He is walking beside us every step of the way. It means what the apostle Paul wrote in Romans 8:28: "And we know that for those who love God all things work together for good, for those who are called according to His purpose." It means what Paul goes on to write about at the end of that chapter, that nothing "will be able to separate us from the love of God in Christ Jesus our Lord" (v. 38). What a promise!

Because we know God is faithful to keep His promises, we can, like the psalmist, "sing [His] praise and not be silent" (Psalm 30:12). We can join the psalmist in saying, "O LORD my God, I will give thanks to You forever." How could we ever be silent when it comes to praise? It seems almost impossible. David could not be silent. He had experienced God's faithfulness. He had received

God's hand of deliverance, and it caused an immediate and heart-felt response. When we finally found our needle-in-the-haystack van, the response was immediate too. We couldn't help but get out of that van and immediately celebrate and praise God for His goodness to us.

You and I have been delivered. We have been and continue to be the recipients of God's faithfulness and goodness. God was faithful to His promise to deliver us from the greatest bondage we have ever known—the bondage of sin, death, and the power of the devil. By His cross and empty tomb, Jesus conquered all these enemies for us. God is and will continue to be faithful to deliver us from our fears, worries, and struggles. No longer are we enslaved, but instead we have been set free by Jesus' life, death, and resurrection. God has traded our clothes of mourning for clothes of joy.

When we got back from that trip, we gave everyone who went along a little piece of that blown-out tire. We glued it to a laminated card that simply said, "God is faithful." The volunteer leaders and I wanted our students to remember that time and God's faithfulness. We wanted them to have something to mark that defining moment of faith in their lives. We wanted them to be able to say in difficult times, "I've been down this road before, and although I'm uncertain of the outcome, I trust in God, who is faithful to walk beside me through it all."

May we also know that God is faithful to hear us when we cry out to Him and is faithful to walk beside us. And through Christ, may we spend a lifetime returning thanks to God, our faithful heavenly Father.

Prayer: Heavenly Father, I praise You for Your faithfulness to hear me when I call out to You. I thank You for Your gift of deliverance and for Your presence with me every step of the journey. You are faithful! I praise You in Jesus' name. Amen.

Friday

Personal Study Questions: Psalm 30:11–12

1. As you read verses 11–12, what kind of celebration or party do you imagine?

2. In the culture of the Old Testament, people wore sackcloth as a sign of deep grief. When mourning the death of a beloved family member, when troubled over a disastrous national defeat in battle, and while in the throes of recognizing sin and repenting over it, people wore this rough, unlovely, uncomfortable clothing. Consider the following meaning of *sackcloth*: How has Jesus "loosed [your] sackcloth"? How has this stirred deep thanksgiving in your heart?

3. Today's faith narrative describes God's faithfulness, deliverance, and goodness using several powerful words and pictures. Which most encourages your faith? Explain.

lisa

Group Bible Study for Week Three
Psalm 30

1. On which day or days this past week did the faith narrative and the reading from Psalm 30 seem pointedly appropriate? Share, as you feel comfortable, why you think so.

2. For what "wonderful deeds" described in Psalm 30 do you especially "give thanks to [the LORD] forever" (v. 12)?

3. At least twice in the past hundred years, novelists have made good use of the imagery from Psalm 30:5, using the title *Joy in the Morning*. In what ways could that same title fit your own life as a child of God?

4. In Psalm 30:7, we read another masterful comparison: "You made my mountain stand strong."

   a. How does the verse say God did this?

   b. To what did the psalmist attribute this strength instead—at least, at first? (See v. 6.)

c. Read Proverbs 2:1–15. These are Solomon's words of advice, wisdom that his father, King David, had passed down to him. How do they reflect the same truths as Psalm 30:6–7?

d. Why, then, do we find it so hard to treasure this wisdom and to base our lives on it rather than on the relative size of our checking account balance or our credit score?

5. Over what challenges and troubles are you "weeping" today (v. 5)? What "joys" would you hope to welcome in "the morning"? Make a list and pray for one another before the members of your group go their separate ways.

Week Four

Psalm 31

1 In You, O Lord, do I take refuge;
let me never be put to shame;
in Your righteousness deliver me!

2 Incline Your ear to me;
rescue me speedily!
Be a rock of refuge for me,
a strong fortress to save me!

3 For You are my rock and my fortress;
and for Your name's sake You lead me
and guide me;

4 You take me out of the net they
have hidden for me,
for You are my refuge.

5 Into Your hand I commit my spirit;
You have redeemed me, O Lord,
faithful God.

6 I hate those who pay regard to
worthless idols,
but I trust in the Lord.

7 I will rejoice and be glad in Your
steadfast love,
because You have seen my affliction;
You have known the distress of my
soul,

8 and You have not delivered me into
the hand of the enemy;
You have set my feet in a broad place.

9 Be gracious to me, O Lord, for I
am in distress;
my eye is wasted from grief;
my soul and my body also.

10 For my life is spent with sorrow,
and my years with sighing;
my strength fails because of my iniquity,
and my bones waste away.

11 Because of all my adversaries I
have become a reproach,
especially to my neighbors,
and an object of dread to my acquaintances;
those who see me in the street flee
from me.

12 I have been forgotten like one
who is dead;
I have become like a broken vessel.

13 For I hear the whispering of
many—
terror on every side!—
as they scheme together against me,
as they plot to take my life.

14 But I trust in You, O Lord;
I say, "You are my God."

15 My times are in Your hand;
rescue me from the hand of my enemies and from my persecutors!

16 Make Your face shine on Your servant;
save me in Your steadfast love!

17 O Lord, let me not be put to
shame,
for I call upon You;
let the wicked be put to shame;
let them go silently to Sheol.

18 Let the lying lips be mute,
which speak insolently against the
righteous
in pride and contempt.

19 Oh, how abundant is Your goodness,
which You have stored up for those
who fear You
and worked for those who take refuge
in You,
in the sight of the children of mankind!

20 In the cover of Your presence You
hide them
from the plots of men;

You store them in Your shelter
from the strife of tongues.

21 Blessed be the Lord,
for He has wondrously shown His
steadfast love to me
when I was in a besieged city.

22 I had said in my alarm,
"I am cut off from Your sight."
But You heard the voice of my pleas
for mercy
when I cried to You for help.

23 Love the Lord, all you His saints!
The Lord preserves the faithful
but abundantly repays the one who
acts in pride.

24 Be strong, and let your heart take
courage,
all you who wait for the Lord!

Judy Henke

Psalm 31:1–5

For You are my rock and my fortress; and for Your name's sake You lead me and guide me.

You Lead Me and Guide Me

 ne of my favorite birthdays was my thirtieth, when I was "kidnapped" by a friend. Two weeks or so before, she told me that on a Friday afternoon I should have my bags packed for a surprise weekend. Intrigued, I eagerly anticipated where we might be going and what we might be doing.

When that Friday finally arrived, she picked me up in her car. The words "Happy 30th" were written with shoe polish on the back windshield. I was surprised, a little embarrassed, and excited about the adventure ahead. As we began driving, I asked questions, trying to guess our destination. It didn't take long for me to realize that we were headed to Chicago to meet up with another good friend. This memorable adventure was filled with excitement of what was yet to come. However, not all unknowns are as thrilling as my birthday trip to Chicago.

Last year, I was hiking one day in a Wisconsin state park with a group of friends, happily walking behind someone else. The beautiful changing leaves signified that autumn was upon us. The air smelled fresh with a hint of wood and moisture. After crossing over a bridge, I unexpectedly realized that I was now the leader of the pack. But I had no idea where I was going! Now I had no one's footsteps to follow as I stepped over logs and brush. I had no one to rely on (or blame) if he or she took a wrong turn. The trail was very narrow and poorly marked. Suddenly, I felt apprehensive for being responsible for the group. How could I lead them if I didn't know what was ahead? What kind of guide would I be if I couldn't show them the right way to go? Although we weren't lost, I felt uneasy just blindly following a narrow and relatively unmarked trail.

This is also how I sometimes feel about the path of my life. I try to plan for the future and dream about what I want my life to be, but many times my plans and dreams don't turn out. I planned to have a job in the business world, then God called me to be a missionary in Thailand for three years. I dreamed about getting married and having children, but God called me to be single. Many times on this path of life, I have felt uneasy because I don't know what lies ahead.

In the first part of Psalm 31, we see that David, too, is uncertain about the path before him. His friends had abandoned him, and he was confronted by a powerful conspiracy. But David calls out to God for help. He takes refuge in the Lord and finds security in Him. How do you find security in a time of uncertainty

Judy

and doubt? How do you keep going when you don't know what lies ahead? These are the times when our faith is tested the most. God is still with us when we don't know what's next or even when we doubt He hears us. I constantly pray David's prayer, "For You are my rock and my fortress; and for Your name's sake You lead me and guide me" (v. 3).

God knows and sees the big picture of our lives. He sees the beginning of our path of life, every twist and turn, and the end. "For [God] formed my inward parts; [He] knitted me together in my mother's womb" (Psalm 139:13). You and I are His precious creations, and He loves us unconditionally.

God knows and sees the big picture of our lives. He sees the beginning of our path of life, every twist and turn, and the end. "For [God] formed my inward parts; [He] knitted me together in my mother's womb" (Psalm 139:13). You and I are His precious creations, and He loves us unconditionally. I know that God specifically formed me and put me in this place and at this time for a reason. Daily I trust that He will lead and guide me along this journey called life and "lead me in the way everlasting" (Psalm 139:24).

But frequently, like David, I get caught in Satan's trap. While hiking in the park, I saw no animal traps nor did I feel trapped in the woods, but in life I often feel trapped by the things of this world. Satan is a master at using my inadequacies, fears, and misgivings to make me doubt my relationship with God. Sometimes when I am lonely and can't feel if God is there, I start to question whether He really is. I not only listen to Satan's lies but actually sometimes believe them! When I realize what the devil—and my sinful flesh—is doing, I quickly try to pray that the Holy Spirit would reassure me of the truth found in God's Word:

"I will not leave you or forsake you" (Joshua 1:5).

"Know therefore that the Lord your God is God, the faithful God who keeps covenant and steadfast love with those who love Him and keep His commandments, to a thousand generations" (Deuteronomy 7:9).

*"And we know that for those who love God
all things work together for good, for those who are
called according to His purpose" (Romans 8:28).*

There are so many verses in the Bible that hold me and uplift me when I feel trapped by the world. Satan knows which buttons to push to make me feel like there is no way of escape. I am bombarded by commercials, TV shows, and movies that communicate what is necessary for a successful and happy life. I eagerly watch and believe what they are telling me: certain products will make me look younger and more attractive, a husband and 2.5 children will make my life complete, this salary and 401k will make everything easier. But that is not what God says! God tells us to keep our eyes on Him, and in Him we will find complete joy and fulfillment. Jesus came to give us life: "I came that they may have life and have it abundantly" (John 10:10). Both fully God and fully man, Jesus paid the ultimate price for our sin. And through His death, He conquered sin, death, and the power of the devil. And now He gives us forgiveness, hope, peace, and eternal life, which we receive through faith.

Each day on this adventure called life, there will be bumps in the road, unknowns ahead, and unexpected twists and turns. But no matter where we are along the path of life, God is there, and He loves and cares for you and me beyond our wildest imagination! Because of His promises in His Word, we believe and trust in Him. This is easier said than done when we're going through rough times. Remember that even while on the cross Jesus quoted David's psalm, completely trusting His Father with His final words, "Into Your hand I commit My spirit" (v. 5). God hears every prayer and answers every plea. So enabled by His Spirit, we, too, *daily* put our spirit into God's hands, trusting that He will lead and guide us according to His good, pleasing, and perfect will, regardless of the twists or turns our paths will take!

Judy

Prayer: Gracious and heavenly Father, thank You for being with me during the difficult times of life and for always being my guide. Please forgive me when I go astray and listen to the lies of Satan. Thank You for giving me Your Word, and help me to stand firm in Your promises. Lead me along this path of life so that along the way others may see Jesus as the way, the truth, and the life. In His precious and holy name. **Amen.**

Sudy

monday

Personal Study Questions: Psalm 31:1–5

1. As in Psalm 30 (and Psalm 18, among many others), David begins Psalm 31 by comparing the Lord to a "rock." He also calls the Lord his "fortress" (vv. 2–3).

   a. Why do you suppose the psalmists so commonly use this comparison?

   b. How does it comfort you—especially in times when the path ahead is none-too-clear?

2. The "net" to which David refers in verse 4 is an image drawn from the custom of hiding a net with a fine mesh on the ground; sprinkling grain, bread crumbs, or other bait across it; and then lying in wait until an unsuspecting quail or another small game bird landed to feed. When it did, the fowler would snap the net, entrapping dinner for himself and his family.

   a. What makes this an apt picture of Satan and his temptations?

   b. When have you recently found yourself snapped up in the net of temptation?

   c. How has your Lord undertaken for you the rescue described in verse 4?

study

Psalm 31:6–10

*I will rejoice and be glad in Your steadfast love, because
You have seen my affliction; You have known the distress
of my soul, and You have not delivered me into the hand
of the enemy; You have set my feet in a broad place.*

A Broad Place

Living in Thailand for three years definitely had a lot of ups and downs. In this tropical country, I was constantly surrounded by beautiful flowers such as orchids, ratchaphruek (the national flower of Thailand), lotus, lilies, and many others. Cut orchids often adorned my kitchen table since colorful bouquets of these purple, pink, and white flowers cost the equivalent of a mere fifty cents in U.S. money. I love fruit, and for me it was wonderful to buy mangos, watermelons, and pineapples year round. Sidewalk vendors sold delicious food from their small carts throughout the city. For lunch or dinner, I often bought kow pad gai

Judy

118

(chicken fried rice), gai pad mamuang himapan (cashew chicken with chilies), pad pak ruam mit (rice with mixed vegetables), tom yam goong (hot and sour spicy shrimp soup), and much more for just fifty cents each! Lacking a car, I often took a taxi, a song tau (pick-up truck with bench seating), a motorcycle taxi, or a bus to get to work, go shopping, or go sightseeing. Compared to means of transportation in the United States, these were cheap; a twenty-minute, 10-mile taxi ride typically cost only about $2. And I could write a book about shopping at JJ Market (also called Chatuchuck Market), where more than 9,000 vendors offer high-quality yet inexpensive items including clothes, gifts, furniture, animals, plants, and much more!

However, living 10,000 miles from home could also be challenging and frustrating. One of the toughest times was when I learned by e-mail that one of my dear church friends in her early forties had a sudden heart attack. I communicated with her husband at the hospital and earnestly prayed for him and their two young children. For a week, it was very difficult to sleep or concentrate, so I prayed and read the Bible. I desperately wanted to be with my church family and offer support to these dear friends, but I couldn't. It was so hard. Although my heart ached each day as I waited for e-mail updates, God gave me tremendous peace about the situation. Just a week after her attack, God called my friend home to be with Him. How I longed to comfort her family, to cry and mourn with them, and to be there to say good-bye. It's hard to describe how difficult it was to be so far away from friends and family during this kind of situation.

I imagine that this is how David felt when he described the "distress of [his] soul" (v. 7). Although his situation was different than mine, the emotions of the human heart are the same throughout all generations. When our souls are in anguish, we can nevertheless experience peace and joy by trusting in the promises of the Lord: "I will rejoice and be glad in Your steadfast love, because You have seen my affliction; You have known the distress of my soul, and You have not delivered me into the hand of the enemy; You have set my feet in a broad place" (vv. 7–8).

Judy

Sometimes this is easier said than done. However, God's Spirit, working through His Word, enables us to remember God's faithfulness in the past and to trust Him with our present and our future. "And those who know Your name put their trust in You, for You, O LORD, have not forsaken those who seek You" (Psalm 9:10).

We can also take comfort in knowing that God will not allow anyone to perish whom He has predestined for salvation: "For those whom He foreknew He also predestined to be conformed to the image of His Son, in order that He might be the firstborn among many brothers. And those whom He predestined He also called, and those whom He called He also justified, and those whom He justified He also glorified" (Romans 8:29–30).

Still today my heart is distressed over the lost. Ninety-five percent of the Thai people are Buddhist, and only one-half of one percent are Christian. There are many temples around the country with gold Buddha statues inside. People revere these idols by placing flowers, incense, and money at their feet. When I traveled in the country with my Thai friends, I grieved as I watched them and many others bow before these statues. Every time I witnessed this scene, I deeply wanted to say, "Buddha cannot help you! There is only one God, and Jesus Christ is the only way to Him! God loved you so much that He sent His Son, Jesus, to die on the cross for your sins and raised Him up on the third day. And by believing in Him you will have forgiveness and eternal life with Him in heaven." I know that shouting that in the middle of a Buddhist temple would not be the best approach, but I was desperate to tell these Thai people the truth.

Of course, Thailand is not the only place where there are lost people. I know there are people living next door and people where I work who don't know Jesus. Every day I talk with international students at the University of Wisconsin who share their thoughts and beliefs about life and religion. One student asked, "Is it better to be good or to believe in God?" Another inquired, "How do you know that the Bible is really true?" Every day I have an opportunity to share the Good News of what Jesus did for us on the cross.

When we are weak with sorrow and grief, whether it be for

Judy

the loss of someone we care about or for people who don't know Jesus, we can still know that God will never leave us or forsake us (Deuteronomy 31:6). We can also take comfort in knowing that despite our inabilities or insecurities about sharing our faith, God will not allow anyone to perish whom He has predestined for salvation: "For those whom [God] foreknew He also predestined to be conformed to the image of His Son, in order that He might be the firstborn among many brothers. And those whom He predestined He also called, and those whom He called He also justified, and those whom He justified He also glorified" (Romans 8:29–30). Satan has no power over us because we belong to Christ; we are His sheep, and He is our Shepherd. "My sheep hear My voice, and I know them, and they follow Me. I give them eternal life, and they will never perish, and no one will snatch them out of My hand. My Father, who has given them to Me, is greater than all, and no one is able to snatch them out of the Father's hand" (John 10:27–29). Just as David was not handed over to the mortal enemy, we will never be handed over to Satan. Instead, God sets our "feet in a broad place" (Psalm 31:8).

Sometimes being afflicted can feel like being bound in chains and unable to get loose. We can be assured that we are not constrained by suffering, pain, and anguish. Instead we are set free by God's amazing grace. Through His Son, God has released us from our enemies of sin, Satan, and death. Standing on the broad place of His forgiveness, we can take comfort in His love and tell others about Jesus.

Prayer: Dear God, we thank You for Your amazing grace. By sending us Your beloved Son, You have shown us Your love. When we suffer anguish, help us to remember Your faithfulness and give us Your peace. Send Your Holy Spirit to comfort us and teach us to rely on You in all circumstances. We ask this for Jesus' sake. Amen.

Judy

121

tuesday

Personal Study Questions: Psalm 31:6–10

1. When have you experienced anguish or distress of the soul like David expressed in verse 7 and that is described in today's faith narrative?

2. Twice in Psalm 31, the psalmist expresses in a direct way his trust in Israel's covenant-making, covenant-keeping God—in verses 6 and 14.

   a. What reasons does the psalm cite for this trust (vv. 7–8)?

   b. What additional reasons can you suggest as you pray the words of the psalm?

3. After reminding himself of the Lord's faithfulness (vv. 1–8), the psalmist brings his need to the throne of grace (vv. 9–10). What makes this a helpful sequence for us as well?

4. How will you use David's approach (remembering, followed by requests) in your own prayer time today?

Psalm 31:11–16

But I trust in You, O LORD; I say, "You are my
God." My times are in Your hand; rescue me from the
hand of my enemies and from my persecutors!

My Times Are in Your Hand

After checking two huge suitcases and wondering if I'd packed the right things, I lugged my 60-pound backpack toward the security area. I was sweating, nervous, and anxious about what lay ahead: a twenty-four-hour flight from St. Louis to Los Angeles to Taipei, Taiwan, then finally to Bangkok, Thailand. I was fairly well-traveled, but I had never flown that far. Would I be able to sleep in the "spacious" coach seating? What movies would they show, and would I be able to see the screen?

Should I take out my contact lenses and hope I didn't lose them?

My sister, brother-in-law, niece, nephew, and several friends, with their smiles and tears, accompanied me at the airport. After I walked through the metal detector, I would not see them for an entire year. A *year!* My parents lived in a different state from my own, and we had already said good-bye a few weeks earlier. I was going to miss soccer games, volleyball matches, dance competitions, and even high school graduation. For this extremely involved aunt, leaving the United States for a year was not going to be easy. In addition, I had so many wonderful friends who had supported, comforted, encouraged, and loved me for many years. Now I was going to a country where I didn't know the language, had no friends, and didn't know the culture (except what I had read on the Internet and in books).

Moving to Thailand wasn't the first time I'd experienced separation. Much to my mother's chagrin, after graduating from university I took a job in a different state, about 350 miles from home. This opportunity was exciting, and I looked forward to living in the same town as my sister and her family. However, I had no friends there yet and didn't know where I would live. A new job, a new home, a new life—such an experience can be overwhelming. But like the writer of Ecclesiastes says, "For everything there is a season, and a time for every matter under heaven" (3:1). During this new season of my life, many of my relationships changed. I lost contact with many of my high school and college friends, but I gained new ones through work, church, and other activities.

I must have felt as David did when he said, "I have become like a broken vessel" (Psalm 31:12). Because of a very strong conspiracy, many of David's friends had abandoned him. But God was faithful to David, just as He is to us. Despite his circumstances, David said, "But I trust in You, O Lord; I say, 'You are my God.' My times are in Your hand" (vv. 14–15).

As I worked as a volunteer missionary in Thailand, God would teach me to depend on Him in ways I never had before. I would come to trust in Him for all my finances and to look to Him to provide friends, skills, and necessities for everyday living.

Judy

124

It seems easy to say, "I trust in You, O Lord." But apart from God's grace in Christ, these words are impossible to say—or believe. But through the Gospel, God enables us to trust in the Lord, to have faith in Him, and to believe His Word. To trust in the Lord means to believe in His promises, to commit ourselves and others to His care, to have confidence in Him, and to rely on Him.

The Lord is my strength and my shield; in Him
my heart trusts, and I am helped; my heart exults,
and with my song I give thanks to Him. Psalm 28:7

In God, whose word I praise, in God I trust;
I shall not be afraid. What can flesh do to me?
Psalm 56:4

O Lord of hosts, blessed is the one who trusts in You!
Psalm 84:12

Whenever I sit in a chair, I trust it will hold me. When I get into my car, I trust it will start. At the end of the month, I trust that I will receive a paycheck. While these are correct statements about trust, they do not mean the same thing as David's "trust" in the verses above. *Trust* is a seemingly little word, yet it has a more profound and deeper meaning. This kind of God-given trust is really more like putting your whole self into His hands.

Before I lived in Thailand, I went on mission trips to Russia, Panama, Venezuela, and Mexico. I also traveled around Europe for six weeks while in college. Most of these trips involved many hours of flying. Thinking about putting myself into God's hands, I have also considered how each time I fly, I put myself into the pilot's hands. I have no fear of flying. Will there be turbulence or bad weather? Will we have to circle around the airport waiting to land? I really don't worry about such things. In fact, sometimes I fall asleep even before we take off. Although I don't know the

Judy

pilot, I am confident in the pilot's ability, and I trust that he or she will bring me safely to my destination. I continue to fly to new destinations and visit family members around the country.

In contrast, I know God because He made Himself known to me, His child, in Baptism. He reveals Himself to me in His Word, which I have read almost all my life. I love God and converse with Him in prayer. Yet, sometimes I don't really trust Him. How can this be? I can trust a pilot I don't know, but I can't trust the God of the universe who loves me, gave me life, sent His Son to die for me, gave me faith, and has an awesome plan for all my days? My sinful nature causes me to doubt God's Word and not to trust Him in all things. So each morning before work, I read His Word and pray to Him. "Let me hear in the morning of Your steadfast love, for in You I trust. Make me know the way I should go, for to You I lift up my soul" (Psalm 143:8). Each morning God reassures me in His Word of His unfailing love for me.

I know God because He made Himself known to me, His child, in Baptism. He reveals Himself to me in His Word, which I have read almost all my life. I love God and converse with Him in prayer.

This is how He feels about you too! Trust in Him with the faith He gave you, and He will show you the way to go. "Trust in the LORD with all your heart, and do not lean on your own understanding. In all your ways acknowledge Him, and He will make straight your paths" (Proverbs 3:5–6). Your paths may not always be the way you think they should go, but God will straighten them for you. God is your trustworthy pilot, and regardless of your destination, your times are in His hand!

Prayer: Dear Lord, You are my strength and my shield. Please forgive me when I fail to trust in You. Time and time again You have shown Your faithfulness to those who seek You. "Make Your face shine on Your servant; save me in Your steadfast love!" (v. 16). I ask this in Jesus' name. **Amen.**

Judy

126

wednesday

Personal Study Questions: Psalm 31:11–16

1. One of David's chief complaints in these verses involves the fact that his neighbors and acquaintances are avoiding him. (See vv. 11–13 and compare Job 19:13–19.) Why are they doing so? When has this ever happened to you?

2. After describing his loneliness, David repeats his words of trust in verse 14. (See v. 6.) This time, we might imagine him stressing the word *you*!

   a. With whom does this "you" contrast?

   b. Scripture everywhere encourages us to trust God; Scripture nowhere urges us to trust other people. What might account for this?

3. Which descriptions from today's faith narrative help you see God's love for you in a new way? Explain.

Psalm 31:17–20

O Lord, let me not be put to shame, for I call upon You;
let the wicked be put to shame; let them go silently to
Sheol. Let the lying lips be mute, which speak insolently
against the righteous in pride and contempt. Oh, how
abundant is Your goodness, which You have stored up
for those who fear You and worked for those who take
refuge in You, in the sight of the children of mankind!

Love Your Enemies

Driving along a two-way street with parking on both sides, I see an open parking space. I look over each shoulder and determine no one is coming in either direction. "Simple," I say to myself, "I'll just slowly reverse into the empty parking space." As I'm backing up, a car appears out of nowhere at a 90-degree angle behind me. I hit it! Moving from a parked position on the opposite side of the street, the driver had swung around and began a u-turn just as I was backing into the empty space.

Judy

The driver calls the police, and we patiently wait for their arrival. Soon, a police car with those lovely red and blue flashing lights appears from around the corner and pulls in behind both our cars. Fortunately, my car wasn't scratched, and the other driver's car was minimally damaged: a slight dent and a partially broken headlight. The policewoman takes both our statements and goes back to her squad car for quite awhile. The other driver is moving to Utah to take a new job. Now he will have to deal with a citation and damage to his car.

After returning with the necessary paperwork, the policewoman presents a ticket. To *me!* What?! How could *I* get a ticket for "unsafe backing"? It was completely safe when I started backing up. *The other driver* did a u-turn from the other side of the street without looking. This was so unfair! In my opinion, a person whipping around from the other side of the street doing a u-turn should be more careful. He was guilty, not I. Being falsely accused, or at least taking all of the blame for something that isn't entirely your fault, is a very hard pill to swallow.

Has anyone ever "stolen" your parking space? Have you ever worked long and hard on a project, after God gave you a brilliant and creative idea, and then someone else took credit for it? In our crazy and sinful world today, people have a way of twisting words, lying, and deceiving in order to advance their careers, make themselves look better, or belittle others. It's times like these that we want to pray with David, "O LORD, let me not be put to shame, for I call upon You; let the wicked be put to shame; let them go silently to Sheol. Let the lying lips be mute, which speak insolently against the righteous in pride and contempt" (vv. 17–18).

When we are faced with these kinds of "enemies" we, like David, can take comfort in knowing that God will deal with people who do not fear and obey Him. Because God will deal justly for us, we respond by following Him, being a servant to others, and proclaiming the truth found in God's Word. "For this is the will of God, that by doing good you should put to silence the ignorance of foolish people" (1 Peter 2:15).

We are all sinful human beings, and not one of us is perfect.

Judy

So we repent of our sins and trust in Jesus alone for our salvation. Through faith, God gives us a heart of compassion and forgiveness, especially for those who do not know Jesus or who do us harm. Jesus told a crowd of His disciples:

> *But I say to you who hear, Love your enemies,*
> *do good to those who hate you, bless those who curse you,*
> *pray for those who abuse you. . . . And if you do good to those who do*
> *good to you, what benefit is that to you? For even sinners do the same.*
> *. . . But love your enemies, and do good, and lend, expecting nothing in*
> *return, and your reward will be great, and you will be sons of the Most*
> *High. . . . Be merciful, even as your Father is merciful.*
> *Luke 6:27–28, 33, 35–36*

For me, this has to be one of the most challenging things in the world to do! My stubborn and always-want-to-be-right sinful nature rejects this concept. Each Easter season I read about what Christ endured for us. Although totally perfect, sinless, and innocent, He was falsely accused, beaten, and ultimately killed by His enemies. He lovingly and willingly bore my sin, your sin, the world's sin—the sin of His enemies—on the cross. When I think about this from a purely human perspective, I can't understand how someone could love their enemies so much that they would give their life for them. And how could God love us so much that Jesus would willingly give up His own life to pay that enormous price for our sin?!

Take heart! God is *that* good! "Oh, how abundant is Your goodness, which You have stored up for those who fear You and worked for those who take refuge in You, in the sight of the children of mankind!" (v. 19). God's goodness, mercy, and grace are evident and available to all who seek Him, fear Him, and take refuge in Him. I am in awe of God's greatness and His love and care for His people. Throughout the Old Testament, we can read how God was frustrated with His people. Yet, then as well as today, He constantly provides and cares for them. When we sincerely repent

Judy

of our sin, He is always there to forgive us and renew us. "Create in me a clean heart, O God, and renew a right spirit within me" (Psalm 51:10). God can and will do this, even as we are confronted by enemies, liars, and deceivers.

Next time you are driving home from work or school and someone cuts you off, pray for that person and watch how it changes your attitude. When you are falsely accused of something, pray that God would teach you how to speak the truth in love and that the other person would somehow be drawn to Christ through the situation. As we focus on God's goodness, trust in His provision, and take shelter under His refuge, He honors His promises, and we see our reproach roll away. God protects and comforts us during all our ordeals. "In the cover of Your presence You hide them from the plots of men; You store them in Your shelter from the strife of tongues" (v. 20).

Although totally perfect, sinless, and innocent, [Jesus] was falsely accused, beaten, and ultimately killed by His enemies.

He lovingly and willingly bore my sin, your sin, the world's sin—the sin of His enemies—on the cross.

Pride has a way of entering our minds and causing us to seek revenge, especially when we have been wronged. By God's grace we can reject that temptation because God provides a shelter of His presence where we can be safe and secure. Paul writes, "Beloved, never avenge yourselves, but leave it to the wrath of God, for it is written, 'Vengeance is Mine, I will repay, says the Lord.' . . . Do not be overcome by evil, but overcome evil with good" (Romans 12:19, 21). So, if someone steals your space or does something even worse, love your enemies. You can rest secure in God's Word and leave the situation in the Lord's hands.

Judy

Prayer: Heavenly Father, when I was your enemy, You sent your Son to die for me so I might be Your friend. Forgive me for not loving my enemies, especially when I have been wronged. Fill me with Your Holy Spirit so I might have a spirit of compassion, forgiveness, and mercy for everyone in my path. For Jesus' sake. *Amen.*

Judy

thursday

Personal Study Questions: Psalm 31:17–20

1. When have you experienced the kinds of unfairnesses described in today's faith narrative and in the psalm verses?

2. How did the Lord "shelter" you and provide a "refuge" for you (vv. 19–20)?

3. For whom might you pray today, asking that the Lord shelter them?

study

Psalm 31:21–24

*Love the LORD, all you His saints! The LORD
preserves the faithful but abundantly repays the
one who acts in pride. Be strong, and let your heart
take courage, all you who wait for the LORD!*

Wait for It

Here is a sight you see almost everywhere: people waiting for a bus. While living in Thailand and being without a car, I often rode a bus. Every morning and afternoon, I stood with many others in 90-degree heat waiting for a bus to arrive. I thought, "The Thai are so patient. How can they be so calm?" I also thought that waiting for a bus could be a good opportunity for God to teach me patience. Day after day, week after week, I observed the Thai and how calm they seem in al-

Judy

134

most every circumstance. However, if they are waiting for a bus, once it arrives they swiftly enter it and eagerly try to find an empty seat or place to stand—so much so that they barely allow riding passengers to disembark! After observing this behavior several times, I spoke with Thai friends about the habits and customs of the Thai people. After a year or so of living in the country, I finally realized the Thai really aren't as patient as I imagined. They just don't show their anger or irritation as readily as we Americans do. The Thai calmly endure heat and humidity, whereas many Americans would complain about the heat or the tardiness of the bus were it not to arrive on time.

Speaking of which, another interesting cultural difference is the Thai attitude toward time. As an American living abroad, I would frequently ask friends if we were on "Thai time" or "American time." "Thai time" meant that we could meet at the specified time or up to an hour following. "American time" (some call it "airport time") would be meeting within five to ten minutes of the specified time. In some ways I like "Thai time" because it is more conducive to the way people live, work, and view life. Although Bangkok is a large city (population ten million), has many businesses, and is influenced by Western culture, life still seems more laid back and relaxed than in the U.S. Because of Bangkok's heavy traffic congestion, walking to a destination is often faster than riding a bus. But alas, people must take the time to wait.

"Please hold while I transfer you to the extension." "Your call will be answered in seven minutes." "Please wait to be seated." In our society, we are still asked to wait for things. We can heat leftovers in the microwave in a matter of minutes, but those few moments seem so long when we are hungry. When a loved one is in surgery, it can seem like an eternity until the doctor gives an update on the progress. If you are thirty-nine years old and waiting to find "Mr. Right," waiting for him to arrive can seem to last forever. Waiting is difficult. During such times, like David we cry out to the Lord that He would hear our cry for mercy (v. 22).

Judy

Think about the children of Israel, who spent centuries in Egyptian bondage, waiting to leave for the Promised Land. Now that's a lot of waiting! Generation after generation, mothers and fathers would teach their children about God's faithfulness to Abraham, Issac, and Jacob, saying that God would deliver them into the Promised Land. Centuries before, the Lord came to Jacob in a dream and said, "Behold, I am with you and will keep you wherever you go, and will bring you back to this land. For I will not leave you until I have done what I have promised you" (Genesis 28:15). Then, some five hundred years later, the Lord commanded Moses to tell the elders of Israel, "I promise that I will bring you up out of the affliction of Egypt to the land of the Canaanites, the Hittites, the Amorites, the Perizzites, the Hivites, and the Jebusites, a land flowing with milk and honey" (Exodus 3:17). After the exodus, the Israelites spent an additional forty years wandering in the desert before they reached the Promised Land. And they weren't patiently waiting! Not that I blame them—frequently I feel like an Israelite because I complain to God about not having enough of *this* or because I want *that*. God, in His forgiving mercy, hears my cry and answers me according to His gracious will.

Since God is not confined by time, He operates on a totally different level than we do. At the same time, He is intimately involved with every detail of our lives. He cares about each one of us!

Even when we can't understand God's ways, we continue to wait and trust in Him. "For My thoughts are not your thoughts, neither are your ways My ways, declares the Lord" (Isaiah 55:8). How could we possibly understand the mind of God? How can we comprehend the intricacies of life and the universe? Since God is not confined by time, He operates on a totally different level than we do. At the same time, He is intimately involved with every detail of our lives. He cares about each one of us! Yes, it is difficult to wait and hope for something without the assurance that what we're waiting for is God's will. That's why we cling to and meditate on His Word, which gives us the assurance we need:

Our soul waits for the Lord;
He is our help and our shield.
Psalm 33:20

Judy

136

I wait for the LORD, my soul waits,
and in His word I hope.
Psalm 130:5

But if we hope for what we do not see,
we wait for it with patience.
Romans 8:25

Waiting for our blessed hope, the appearing of the glory of our great
God and Savior Jesus Christ, who gave Himself for us to redeem us
from all lawlessness and to purify for Himself a people for His own
possession who are zealous for good works.
Titus 2:13–14

How do we hope and wait patiently at the same time? These are God's gifts to us through faith. God has shown His wonderful love to us through sending us His Son, Jesus Christ. He is faithful to His children. Just because we don't always get the results we expect doesn't mean that God isn't listening to our cries. God waits patiently for us to lean on Him and really see Him as our "Abba," our Father in heaven. He yearns for us to seek Him with all our heart, soul, mind, and strength (Mark 12:30). Then we will find that He has been with us, beside us, all along.

David tells us to "Love the LORD, all you His saints! The LORD preserves the faithful but abundantly repays the one who acts in pride" (v. 23). The Lord will preserve us as we deal with life's difficult issues. He is our deliverer, our comforter, our refuge, our rock, and our fortress. God has called us to be His own; Jesus has purchased us through the power of His blood on the cross. We can confidently and assuredly wait on the Lord and put our hope in Him. And when our fleeting life is over, we will no longer have to wait, for we will live with Him forever in heaven.

David's psalm puts it best: "Be strong, and let your heart take courage, all you who wait for the LORD!" (v. 24).

Judy

Prayer: Dear Jesus, my joy and hope are found in You. Please forgive me for being impatient with others, with myself, and with You. You care about every detail of my life and have listened to my cries for help. Thank You that my times are in Your hands. May Your name be praised. **Amen.**

Sudy

Personal Study Questions:
Psalm 31:21–24

1. What contrasts do you note in verse 22 between feelings and reality?

2. Reread David's encouragements to you In verses 23–24. He has expressed these in words so personal we can almost imagine ourselves sitting across the table from him, chatting over a cup of coffee and a bagel!

   a. How do these words—God's Word—strengthen and embolden you right now?

   b. How can they help you wait more patiently for those things for which you have already prayed a long time?

Study

Group Bible Study for Week Four
Psalm 31

1. Sometimes as we encounter problems or challenges, well-meaning friends will say, "I know just how you feel." Really, though, they don't. They can't. They aren't us; they do not have our set of past experiences, our temperament, our outlook on life, our unique combination of strengths and weaknesses. Yet Psalm 31 reveals the truth that our Lord really does know how we feel. He has inspired the psalmists to write the very words we can pray to encourage ourselves when we face any of life's troublesome situations.

   a. Which verses in the psalm describe the experiences our Lord Jesus endured during His time here on earth?

   b. In what kinds of situations will you return to Psalm 31 in the future for comfort and help?

2. How did you grow in both knowledge and trust this week as you studied Psalm 31? Explain.

3. Someone has said that Psalm 31 takes the reader "from gloom to glory." In what ways is that an apt description?

4. While David touches on many topics, mentioning many needs, the theme that ties the psalm together and keeps it flowing forward is God's faithfulness and David's reliance on it.

a. When do your prayers resemble David's—jumping from one need, hurt, and statement of faith to the next?

b. Why did David pray this way? Why do you?

c. How does David avoid over-familiarity and flippant disrespect?

d. Why is this important?

5. Which faith narrative from the past week did you find most helpful, insightful, or encouraging? Explain.

Week Five

Psalm 32

¹ Blessed is the one whose transgression is forgiven,
whose sin is covered.

² Blessed is the man against whom the LORD counts no
iniquity,
and in whose spirit there is no deceit.

³ For when I kept silent, my bones wasted away
through my groaning all day long.

⁴ For day and night Your hand was heavy upon me;
my strength was dried up as by the heat of summer. *Selah*

⁵ I acknowledged my sin to You,
and I did not cover my iniquity;
I said, "I will confess my transgressions to the LORD,"
and You forgave the iniquity of my sin. *Selah*

⁶ Therefore let everyone who is godly
offer prayer to You at a time when You may be found;
surely in the rush of great waters,
they shall not reach him.

^{7} You are a hiding place for me;
You preserve me from trouble;
You surround me with shouts of deliverance. *Selah*

^{8} I will instruct you and teach you in the way you should go;
I will counsel you with my eye upon you.

^{9} Be not like a horse or a mule, without understanding,
which must be curbed with bit and bridle,
or it will not stay near you.

^{10} Many are the sorrows of the wicked,
but steadfast love surrounds the one who trusts in the Lord.

^{11} Be glad in the Lord, and rejoice, O righteous,
and shout for joy, all you upright in heart!

Jill Hasstedt

Psalm 32:1–4

*Blessed is the one whose transgression is forgiven,
whose sin is covered. Blessed is the man against whom
the Lord counts no iniquity, and in whose spirit there is no deceit.*

You Are Blessed

I have a secret passion for television medical dramas. Over the years, I have noticed a familiar plot line involving hysterical blindness. Early in the episode, viewers are introduced to a beautiful, young accident victim who awakens blind from a coma. Medical personnel find no physical reason for her new disability. Viewers soon learn that the victim has witnessed a terrible event and that her blindness is caused by her mind's inability to deal with it. Never fear, in less than forty-five minutes, the

hero, a handsome physician, discovers the traumatic cause of her affliction and helps her to regain her sight. I love happy endings! (Okay! Okay! I'll also admit to a having a soft spot for handsome doctors who help beautiful patients. Sigh!)

Doctors refer to hysterical blindness as a dissociative disorder. Apparently a classic symptom is *la belle indifference*—the notable lack of concern seen in the sufferers. Physical blindness manifests itself among some patients who do not want to see something too painful to accept. While it doesn't mention hysterical blindness, Psalm 32 does inform us about a form of spiritual blindness. This psalm is a teaching psalm (maskil) about a sinner's journey of repentance. It is a twin to Psalm 51 and is thought to have been written after David's adultery with Bathsheba, the murder of Uriah, the death of innocent bystanders, and the loss of their first child (see 2 Samuel 11–12).

David begins Psalm 32 with the happy ending. In verses 1 and 2, he writes gratefully of God's forgiveness. He knows what it is to be blessed. Incredibly, David's terrible sins are now "forgiven," "covered," and "not counted against him." However, in later verses, David also reveals the path he followed into a kind of spiritual hysterical blindness. Surely, he knew what he deserved for his manipulative and immoral actions. Was it his fear of God's wrath or his own deep shame that made him keep silent for almost a year? David says his "bones wasted" and that he was "groaning all day long;" God's "hand was heavy upon" him and his "strength was dried up."

Before forgiveness comes, we need a dose of reality. God's Law acts as a mirror that reflects our sins back into our faces. At some point, David stopped lying to himself and to God. He saw his sin. Because of the promised Messiah who would pay for David's sin—and ours—by shedding His precious blood on the cross, David experienced forgiveness and learned the heart-lifting joy of being someone "in whose spirit there is no deceit" (v. 2). Christ's blood is the costly cure for spiritual hysterical blindness that we receive at no cost to us—a cure received by faith that gives us new spiritual eyes.

When it comes to my own blindness to sin, I have discovered, like David, that a great deal of pain often comes before God's Law gets my attention. Eventually, it breaks my indifference and enables me to see the real problem—me. Why couldn't I have been born less stubborn? Only hindsight has allowed me to see where I have been spiritually blind to God's will. Unfortunately, a lack of foresight is not an excuse for sin.

When it comes to my own blindness to sin, I have discovered, like David, that a great deal of pain often comes before God's Law gets my attention. Eventually, it breaks my indifference and enables me to see the real problem—me.

For me, not connecting my sin to its results coincided with the interminable adolescent years of one of my sons. Our relationship was getting steadily worse, and I was totally focused on him as the problem. To be brutally honest and with "no deceit" (after all, I am trying to learn from David's example here), I can see now what I didn't see then. I thought there was something wrong with him and if I could fix him or fix what I thought were his problems, then life would get better for the whole family. So, a great deal of my physical, emotional, and even spiritual energy was poured into "fixing." Perhaps you are starting to see my problem. I didn't. I was blind. I had not figured out that it does not work to look at external causes for an internal problem. I was going after the speck of sawdust in my son's eye rather then the huge wooden plank in my own (Matthew 7:3). Life was not pretty! That plank made it very hard to see. Walking around with a board sticking out of the front of your head can be injurious to others.

In the midst of all that parenting pain, my mom was dying slowly from Alzheimer's disease. I had a conflicted relationship with Mom during my own adolescent years that continued well into adulthood. It was difficult to bear what I perceived as her constant criticism. Our relationship survived, but the scars remained. I believe that the Lord used the long good-bye of Alzheimer's to give me the time He knew I needed to learn to love her as He loves me—as is. Mom and I forgave one another. The Holy Spirit was making good come from bad as He used pain and experience to teach wisdom. I became less critical of her as a parent and as a woman. After all, I obviously wasn't so hot at the whole parenting game myself. Certainly, there were times when God's hand was "heavy upon me" (v. 4), just as David describes.

My blindness started to dissolve. I came to see that I had been hypercritical as a daughter. Was I also hypercritical as a mother? Was the thing I had despised most in my relationship with my mother the same sin that I had carried into my own parenting? God even sent me someone who said these very words, "We hate most in others what we see in ourselves." Ouch!

Those years were miserable in many ways. I believed that despite all my effort, I was failing at the most important job God has ever given me. I saw my failures as a daughter and as a mother. There were even the physical symptoms of stress (acid reflux); anxiety (panic attacks); and the same strength sapping (depression) that David describes in verses 3–4. The future did not look pretty. I could see only doom ahead, and my heart was breaking.

Thankfully, the story doesn't end here, although today's narrative does. God can do amazing things with a broken heart! For now, hold on to the beautiful ending that David gives witness to in verses 1–2 as he celebrates the lighthearted happiness of one who fully experiences the grace of God.

If you are burdened by the weight of sin in your life, turn to Jesus. Look at God's Law, then look to Christ's cross. God has a plan for your life, and His plans are always perfect. Trust in the One who promises to be present with you always (Matthew 28:20). Know that nothing can separate you from the love of God in Christ Jesus (Romans 8:37–39). Indeed, Jesus is your Great Physician, who restores your spiritual sight. You are blessed, because by His cross your transgression is forgiven, your sin is covered.

Prayer: Heavenly Father, I, too, am spiritually blind. Open my eyes to Your Law in my life and my need for a Savior. Through the blood of Your Son, grant me the new spiritual eyes of faith, so I may delight in Your will and gladly serve those You place in my life. In Jesus' name. *Amen.*

monday

Personal Study Questions: Psalm 32:1–4

1. Those who categorize the Psalms, usually list Psalm 32 with five other "penitential" psalms: 38, 51, 102, 130, and 143.

   a. How do the first four verses of Psalm 32 hint at the whole psalm's penitential nature?

   b. What synonyms for *forgiveness* do you find in the first two verses?

2. God's forgiveness puts us into a state of "blessedness." So, too, does a spirit in which there is "no deceit" (v. 2).

   a. What clues do you take from verse 3 and from today's faith narrative as to what this deceit involves?

   b. Someone has said, "You can't fool God." Why might we want to try, though?

   c. The saying goes on: "You can't fool God, and you don't have to!" How does Psalm 32 assure us of the good news that we need not hide our sins from God in the ways David evidently tried at first to do?

Psalm 32:5

I acknowledged my sin to You, and I did not cover my iniquity; I said, "I will confess my transgressions to the Lord," and You forgave the iniquity of my sin. Selah

Jesus, Savior, Wash Away

Aunt Ruth and Uncle Les used to take my twin brother and me to their farm for annual vacations. We loved every minute of barn-exploring, kitten-finding, pig-watching fun! One morning when we were just six or seven years old, we awakened early and headed downstairs to wait for Aunt Ruth to prepare breakfast. While we played, we accidentally knocked over a small planter, spilling dirt across the kitchen table's Formica top. Our solution was simple. We righted the planter and brushed all the dirt to the floor so Aunt Ruth would not see it. Then we put on our best innocent faces and waited. Needless to say, our cover-up did not work. The dirt we thought we had so cleverly brushed aside was still clearly visible all around our feet. Confronted with the evidence, we confessed and were quickly guided in the proper usage of a dustpan and broom.

Verse 5 is David's admission that his cover-up had not worked either. He acknowledged his sin. *Acknowledge* is an interesting word. It can refer to the acquisition of knowledge—as in, you did not have the knowledge before but now you have that knowledge. It can also refer to the admission of knowledge—as in, you admit that you already knew something to be true but now you are definitely saying so. Was David blind until the pain in his life caused him to acquire the insight that allowed him to see his sin? Or did David simply finally admit to knowing that he had been sinning all along? A bit of both may have been involved. What matters is that, finally, he did admit to every wrongdoing.

The acknowledgment of sin matters to God because it makes an eternal difference for us. David was sinful; he was guilty of murder in the first degree. Uriah was dead, and a few other men were killed in David's plot, making him directly responsible for their deaths as well. We're sinful too. Oops. You may cringe at my calling you or even myself sinful. You may think that is harsh. Surely serial killers and terrorist torturers are sinful . . . not us. We just make mistakes or get lost in a few bad decisions. That's not really sin . . . right?

Wrong. Let's define sin, but first let's admit it exists. Something is not right about a world where people blow each other up, where innocents are abused, and where love fails. Sin is everything that acts against God's perfect and holy will. God is Creator. Sin is a destroyer. It causes harm, misfortune, and destruction.

God did not intend for us humans to know sin. The evil present in our world is a result of our rebellion against Him (Genesis 3:6–7). The devil was the first of God's creatures to rebel. Jesus called him "the father of lies" (John 8:44). Perhaps the most effective lie Satan ever devised is that he does not exist and that we are not really all that sinful! We just make "mistakes." That might sound better to us, but it doesn't fool God.

God's original design was a paradise of peace. Humans sinned by disbelieving God and by disobeying His Word. Through Adam and Eve's sin, all of creation began to suffer. We can experience the consequences of sin in our world due to no fault of our own. A drunken driver kills a father. A tornado destroys a family home. A flood or fire sweeps away a neighborhood. Suffering these things does not mean the victim is to blame.

Forgiveness is not something I achieve by being penitent. It is God's gift to me achieved by Christ's redemptive action on my behalf. Through His death and resurrection, God "forgave the iniquity of my sin" (v. 5).

However, sometimes we suffer the consequences due to our own sin. We have control, and it is our fault. Our thoughts, words, and actions miss the mark of God's original and perfect plan. Remember, sin causes harm, misfortune, and destruction. So if my thoughts, words, or deeds cause harm or misfortune or are destructive to myself or to others, then that is . . . well . . . sin. Calling sin by softer words is ultimately an attempt to cover it up. That's a flag that won't fly before the eyes of a perfect and holy God. Our heavenly Father is even smarter than my Aunt Ruth, and the dirt is still visible.

The Book of Ezekiel talks about God's promise to give the nation of Israel a new heart (Ezekiel 11:19; 36:26). He said He would turn their "heart of stone" into a "heart of flesh." A new heart is a softer heart. Unlike the old heart of stone, a new heart is pliable and teachable. A soft heart may seem weaker than a stone heart, but God has that angle covered as well. God's Spirit helps us when we are weak (Romans 8:26); indeed God's power "is made perfect in weakness" (2 Corinthians 12:9).

When David showed true remorse, he experienced God's lavish love and the richness of His forgiveness. Psalm 51 also testifies to what David learned. What pleases God more than sacrifices is "a broken and contrite heart" (51:17). David goes on to say, "Create in me a clean heart, O God, and renew a right spirit

within me" (51:10). Only God can transform a heart from hard to soft, from broken to whole, from dirty to clean, and make a totally new person for it to beat within.

As we ponder the remainder of this psalm, it is good to reflect again on verses 1–2. The triune God who created us in love also re-creates us! Forgiveness is not something I achieve by being penitent. It is God's gift to me achieved by Christ's redemptive action on my behalf. Through His death and resurrection, God "forgave the iniquity of my sin" (v. 5). I receive this precious gift through faith, as God's Spirit turns my life in a new direction. God unpacks the guilt and provides the strength and wisdom for the repacking required for the new adventure He has in store.

Despite Mom's Alzheimer's, God granted me many sweet moments with her before He took her home to be with Him. As my heart softened, I began to remember and savor all the ways she had blessed me. The first Bible stories I ever heard were heard on her lap. Her hands were the first to help mine fold in prayer. She sang in the kitchen, teaching me that I was Jesus' little lamb. She gave me my first Bible. I remembered that I had accompanied her on visits to the elderly and watched her exercise an extraordinary spiritual gift for mercy. I have seen evidence of some of her loveliest traits lived out in my sons as well.

The Lord can indeed do amazing things with broken hearts. At the end of her journey in this life, there was just one thing left between my Mom and me—love. All that other clutter was gone. Her final gift to her family was the comforting certainty that her soul was with Jesus in heaven. My last prayer at her bedside was the one she had first taught me as a little girl.

Jesus, Savior, wash away
All that has been wrong today;
Help me every day to be
Good and gentle, more like Thee.

Prayer: Heavenly Father, I acknowledge my sins before You, those I can recall, as well as those I cannot. For the sake of my Savior, Jesus Christ, wash away all my sin. Turn my heart of stone into a heart of flesh, so I might glorify You in everything I say and do. **Amen.**

Personal Study Questions: Psalm 32:5

1. The psalmist "uncovered" his sin by confessing it. Evidently, he struggled with this for quite a long while before he did so.

   a. What evidence of that struggle do you read in verses 3–4?

   b. When have you participated in a similar struggle?

   c. Verse 5 gives no evidence that in the end David bemoaned his sin in a confession that lasted for hours. Instead, he simply "acknowledged" it. How did the Lord respond?

2. Sometimes even those who have known Jesus and the Gospel message of His cross for many decades believe that for "especially bad" sins, we must feel terrible, moping through our lives for several days before receiving the pardon the Lord offers and the joy that flows from it. How does verse 5 debunk that myth? See also 1 John 1:9.

3. Today's faith narrative says, "The Lord can indeed do amazing things with broken hearts." What evidence of that does the author cite? What evidence from your own life can you add?

Psalm 32:6–7

Therefore let everyone who is godly offer prayer to You at a time when You may be found; surely in the rush of great waters, they shall not reach him. You are a hiding place for me; You preserve me from trouble; You surround me with shouts of deliverance. Selah

You Are a Hiding Place

Last summer I met my first screaming monkey! We were introduced at a bookstore while I attended a national gathering for Christian teenagers. One monkey flew straight at me, flung by a mischievous friend. These small stuffed monkeys equipped with slingshot arms have an internal device that makes a loud screaming noise as they fly through the air. Guided by some helpful teens, it took only moments to learn how to launch my own screaming monkey. I purchased three of them before I left the store.

Screaming monkeys were great conversation starters. Once I learned how to make my monkey fly through the air, I wanted everyone else to have the same experience. I found it easy to tell perfect strangers all about this amazing toy and found myself shooting my monkey across hotel lobbies, restaurants, and airport terminals in the days that followed. My monkey even showed up at my church in a Sunday morning children's message about witnessing. (Don't worry. I collaborated with my pastor in advance, and the monkey flew safely across the church without hitting a single elder. Phew!) The point was this: if it was so easy to tell strangers about the joy of a new toy, why couldn't we share the joy of our salvation like that? Jesus is so much better than a screaming monkey!

Verse 6 of our psalm begins with the word *Therefore*. This one word signifies a change in the psalm's focus. David redirects his attention from himself to the worshipers. In effect, he is saying, "Because of all I've learned, I have some important lessons I can share with you." Once David had experienced the joy and peace that comes after forgiveness, he had to do something with that experience. Perhaps the Lord could use him to warn others and prevent similar tragedies.

David's "Therefore" is followed by an even bigger statement: "let everyone who is godly offer prayer to You at a time when You may be found" (v. 6). Can't you just see the urgency of David's heart for others to acknowledge sin and experience forgiveness? Life is short. There is a time when God may be found, but there is also a time when it will be too late. Don't wait! It's too risky. John the Baptist had it right—"Repent, for the kingdom of heaven is at hand" (Matthew 3:2).

I was in New Orleans the weekend Hurricane Katrina hit. After watching the news on Saturday morning, a friend and I attending the same meeting made a quick call to change our flights. We must have been among the first to do so because the airline seemed surprised at our request. No one thought Katrina would actually hit New Orleans. After consulting the weather reports, they agreed to move our flight to Sunday morning instead of

Sunday afternoon. By Saturday night, it was clear that the city would be in the hurricane's path. We decided to leave the hotel at 2 a.m. for our late morning flight, fearing the thirty-minute trip could take hours in evacuation traffic. The taxi driver got a huge tip that morning. We were grateful that he had stayed to work so we could get to safety. The airport was chaotic, and the atmosphere was anxious and uneasy. I called my church and asked for prayer, knowing that God sometimes waits to act until we ask for His help. I was asking! How reassuring to know my faith family was praying too!

I left friends and strangers behind in New Orleans, knowing time was running out for them. But every day, there are friends, family members, and strangers in our path for whom time is running out. God can use us in a variety of ways to share the Gospel.

Our flight was among the last to leave before the airport closed. I should have felt relieved to be leaving, and I did, but I also felt sick for those who were not getting out. It felt wrong to leave. My friends and I had tried offering our seats to other passengers, but the airline told us they could not use our tickets. The authorities made it clear that it was our duty to leave. They did not need more potential victims to rescue. The days ahead would see our worst fears come true.

Incredibly, during those hard days I learned to have a heart for people who were far from the Lord. (This is an almost laughable statement coming from a woman who once asked the Lord for any spiritual gift as long as it *wasn't* the gift of evangelism.) I left friends and strangers behind in New Orleans, knowing time was running out for them. But every day, there are friends, family members, and strangers in our path for whom time is running out. God can use us in a variety of ways to share the Gospel. I keep asking God to make me be like that taxi driver, willing to stay at my post as long as possible so others can get to safety.

It is interesting that David exhorts the "godly" in verse 6. It seems a bit as if he might be preaching to the choir. Like my New Orleans experience, he uses the powerful imagery of rising flood waters. The worshipers he was speaking about would have understood this reference as a depiction of chaos, threat, and death. David knew the "godly" were in peril. Believers are not free

from temptation and sin on this side of heaven. It has even been suggested that the devil puts greater effort into tempting believers because he already has the other guys. Surely he attempts to isolate us from our heavenly Father. David knew the Lord, but he walked away. Now he sounds the warning to all present, "You are not immune!"

The psalm continues, "You are a hiding place for me; You preserve me from trouble; You surround me with shouts of deliverance" (v. 7). Oh, how good it is to trust the heavenly Father, who forgives us for the sake of His Son. He will not fail us when even the worst disaster comes. I left thirteen friends behind that day in New Orleans. I was deeply relieved and celebrated when the news of their rescue came. However, they were all believers, and had they not been rescued from the aftermath of Katrina, they would still have been safe in heaven, and there would still have been a reason to celebrate.

Verse 7 ends, "You surround me with shouts of deliverance." Being surrounded implies the presence of others. "Shouts" is plural, implying more than one song or more than one singer. This line made me think of Jesus' words in His parable of the lost coin: "Just so, I tell you, there is joy before the angels of God over one sinner who repents" (Luke 15:10). Daily we repent and trust in God's mercy for Christ's sake. We depend upon the Holy Spirit's sanctifying power to accomplish the makeover we cannot accomplish ourselves. Our heavenly Father rejoices in the presence of the angels over you, me, and all sinners who repent and trust in Christ. Enjoy it! Bask in it! And be ready too! This is no monkey business. God is our hiding place. Your Creator, Redeemer, and Sanctifier has great plans for you!

Prayer: Lord God, You desire all to come to repentance and faith. Help me to recognize those opportunities You place before me when I can share with others Your salvation and mercy through Jesus Christ, our Lord. In His name I pray. Amen.

Personal Study Questions:
Psalm 32:6–7

1. How does the "Therefore" at the beginning of verse 6 tie verses 6–7 to verse 5?

2. No one knows for sure, but Bible scholars have suggested that *Selah* was a term that signaled a musical interlude, giving worshipers time to pause and ponder the truth they had just heard or sung. If that's true, why is the *Selah* placed between verses 7 and 8 especially appropriate?

3. What insight does today's faith narrative draw from the fact that verse 7 refers to songs or shouts (plural) of deliverance?

Psalm 32:8–9

I will instruct you and teach you in the way you should go; I will counsel you with My eye upon you. Be not like a horse or a mule, without understanding, which must be curbed with bit and bridle, or it will not stay near you.

Neither Bit nor Bridle

Money was short. When we moved from a lower-cost housing market to another state where homes were much more expensive, we were left with little choice but to buy a fixer-upper. Over the next three years, we spent most of our money and spare time on doing just that. We had help. One November weekend, my parents came to stay with us so my dad and my husband, Fred, could re-move the old rotten sliding patio door and replace it with a new one that promised to be airtight for the winter days ahead.

Did I mention that both my dad and my husband were ac-complished "do it yourselfers" who felt little need to read direc-tions? They teased me for carefully laying out the directions and sitting down to read them as they began their task. After all, what could I possibly contribute? Had I ever replaced a patio door? (They never had either, but that was considered an irrelevant detail.) They almost had me convinced. However, having watched these two wonderful men in my life do projects before, I figured it wouldn't hurt to be informed. So, I read the directions.

Since I didn't want to be a nag and since Mom and I had meals to prepare and children to care for, it was almost dusk be-fore I realized that the house was quite cold and there was still a half-installed door in an open wall of my house. I noticed Dad and Fred both looked frustrated. They explained that the door just wasn't working right and wondered if we needed to take it back to the home improvement store.

After checking the directions one more time, I bravely of-fered comment, "Guys, I think you've been trying to put the door in upside down." There was silence as they both slowly ventured to the table to peek over my shoulder at the despised instruction manual. Much groaning and laughter followed as they realized that was indeed the problem and hurried to install it correctly before dark. Dad is at home in heaven now, where I am sure there is no need for instruction manuals, instruments of the devil that they are, but Fred and I still chuckle over that November after-noon.

David writes in verse 8 of our psalm, "I will instruct you and teach you in the way you should go; I will counsel you with My eye upon you." This bit of godly instruction is God's way of allowing David to quote Him directly. For himself, David seems to be saying, "Look I tried it on my own. I did not follow God's in-structions (the Law). I learned the hard way, and I paid a terrible price. I want you to avoid my mistakes. Listen to the Lord, whose instructions are always perfect, and who gives wise counsel, who will be there watching over you."

David says, "Be not like a horse or a mule, without understanding, which must be curbed with bit and bridle" (v. 9).

By His grace, we who have been made the daughters of God in our Baptism are given the right to ask Him for anything that is good. Jesus promises that our prayers will be heard and answered.

My maiden name is Muehlfelt (pronounced MULE-felt). It's a German name, and our parents were certain that our cultural DNA had predisposed us to stubbornness. With five children to raise, Mom would occasionally come to the end of her patience with her strong-willed brood. I knew I was in deep trouble if I heard my full name with a twist, "Jill Ann Mule-*hide*!" I could relax a bit if this treatment was instead applied to a sibling. The "Mule-hide" adaptation was a reference to our thick-skinned ability to ignore instruction. When I married, my last name changed to Hasstedt. Some of you with sharp eyes may note that there is a reference to the donkey family within this name as well. (That is so unfair!)

Animals think, but they cannot "think about thinking." They were not created as we were in God's image (Genesis 1:27), with a soul, having received the very breath of God (Genesis 2:7). Horses and mules are forced to conform to their master's will by the use of a bit and bridle. Shouldn't we be wiser? We have what animals do not. We have some natural understanding of God's will for us, even if our natural, stubborn, sinful tendency is to ignore that. By faith, I know God's wisdom is greater than my own. By faith, I also know about God's mercy through the suffering and resurrection of our Savior. So shouldn't my heart be more open to His will? Yes. It should. But I have learned to my personal chagrin that I am still "Jill Ann Mule-hide" at heart. I passed this tendency to my children. It makes me want to bray . . . oops, I mean "pray" every day that they will have the wisdom I have often not had in being open and obedient to God's will for their lives.

What if your heart aches as mine has when a loved one is acting quite mulish? I do not intend to give the impression in the

Jill

previous paragraph that I take prayer lightly. What is prayer but "coming to God!" I have learned not to hesitate to go to the Lord. The Bible gives us multiple examples of God waiting until His people called upon Him before He acted on their behalf. In Genesis 18–19, Abraham's conversations with God are startling. This section of Scripture gives evidence that the Lord reveals His purposes to His people, hears their intercession on behalf of others, and will choose to act on behalf of that intercession. Jesus makes the same point in Matthew 7:7–11 when He tells us to ask, seek, and knock. Any good Bible commentary you consult on this passage will note that the present imperative form of the Greek here refers to persistence and intensity. In other words, when it comes to prayer, we are to "Keep asking!" "Keep seeking!" and "Keep knocking!"

By His grace, we who have been made the daughters of God in our Baptism are given the right to ask Him for anything that is good. Jesus promises that our prayers will be heard and answered. I trust that even if I do not see the answer right away, the Lord Himself is on it, applying His perfect wisdom and timing to the matter. I pray. He answers . . . somehow, someday, perfectly.

I have also learned this truth: don't just pray alone! Jesus tells us in Matthew 18:19–20 that if two people on earth agree about what to ask for, it will be done for them. In some mysterious way, when God's people gather for prayer with two or with even just one other person, Jesus is present right there with them. I believe with all my heart that God uses His Word to show me His will. I respond to His will by my prayer. Only my stubborn, sinful mule-hide would turn away from such strength, wisdom, and transformative power. He comes to me and brings me to Him not with bit or bridle but through love alone. Dear sister, God's eye is upon you. Through His Word, He will "instruct you and teach you in the way you should go" (v. 8).

Prayer: Gracious God, You know I try to hide behind my stubborn pride. Help me to realize that You are always watching out for me and that through Your Word, You are leading me on the right path, the path of Christ's righteousness. In Jesus' name. **Amen.**

thursday

Personal Study Questions:
Psalm 32:8–9

1. At first blush, these verses may feel somewhat "stuck on," a kind of afterthought that may not play an integral part in the text. In reality, though, David here adds one more argument to his advice that we be "quick to repent, quick to confess." Based on the patio door story from today's faith narrative, how would you summarize that argument?

2. Have you ever lived—like a horse or mule—in stubborn rebellion for a period of time? If so, what was it like? If not, what clues do you see in verses 3–4 to tell you what it might be like?

3. What will you say to Jesus, your Savior, today as you consider His work to make your pardon possible?

Psalm 32:10–11

*Many are the sorrows of the wicked, but steadfast
love surrounds the one who trusts in the LORD.
Be glad in the LORD, and rejoice, O righteous,
and shout for joy, all you upright in heart!*

Shout for Joy

"Willie, Willie, Willie Woops!"
When I was three or four,
that is what my dad would
call out as he pretended
to toss me in the air. He
would do this once, twice,
and then finally, on the
third "Willie" he would
throw me high above his head, catching me safely in his
arms as I descended. (Willie was a nickname he used for
me at his more mischievous moments even into my adulthood.) This game could be easily initiated by running to

greet him at the back door when he arrived home from work.

There is no fear associated with those precious memories of childhood, only the thrill of being tossed into the air and the complete trust that my father's love would not allow me to fall. My father loved me. I knew that. His love was just there. I never had to think about it, just as I never had to think about whether he would catch me. It happened, always, without fail.

Such trusting, childlike faith often disappears as life teaches hard lessons of threat, loss, and failure. We grow up and we learn the world is not a safe place and that others cannot always be trusted. More heartbreaking to me is the thought that not everyone had a dad like mine. Many people grow up without experiencing the joy of a secure and healthy bond with a loving parent. When real life hits hard, some even come to blame God for failing them—for not being there to stop a tragedy, heal a disease, or protect a child. I've been mad at God a time or two as well, but I think the blame is misplaced.

I have come to understand that the problem of tragedy and loss and hardship in the world and in my life is not due to a disinterested God who sits back and watches things happen. The God of John 3:16 is not a distant figure lacking a heart for His people. Rather, He is the loving heavenly Father, who sent His Son to die for me and for you. His Son is Jesus, Immanuel, God with us. He is God with me—with you.

The shortest passage in the Bible is "Jesus wept" (John 11:35). The full context of the verse is worth reading (vv. 17–44). Upon hearing of the death of His friend Lazarus, Jesus shed tears. Seeing this, those around Him had two reactions. Some saw His tears as evidence of His love. Others saw His tears and wondered if they were evidence of something else. After all, if He could heal a blind man, couldn't He have prevented the death of His friend? Can you hear those same two arguments today as people question God's action or lack of it in life's circumstances? If God is all-powerful, why didn't He do something?!

I once heard a theologian refer to Lazarus as the first Christian martyr. He commented that although this designation is usually given to Stephen, who was stoned to death (Acts 7:54–60), Stephen had given up only his life for Jesus. Lazarus gave up heaven—at least for a time. Is that the real reason Jesus wept for His friend?

On this side of heaven, we'll never know with certainty why Jesus wept. We know that He prayed aloud to His Father so people might believe God sent Him (John 11:41–42). For me it all boils down to faith. What shall I believe? Shall I believe that Jesus chose not to save His friend, or shall I believe that God's purposes were accomplished in some bigger way because the events occurred the way they did? Hmmm. Do I choose to be angry over my evaluation of God's apparent inaction, or do I choose to trust that He cares and is surely involved somehow? I'm not going to go into a big theological treatise here on the problem of sin and evil in the world and where the blame belongs. I know about sin, and I know that human choice set it in motion. I know that I suffer for my own sin and that sometimes I suffer for the sin of others. I even understand that when natural disasters (earthquakes, tornadoes, floods, etc.) or physical calamities (cancer, stroke, arthritis, etc.) dump themselves upon humankind that those things too are the results of sin that now mar God's perfect creation. I hate that, but I also hear the Word of God telling me over and over again that Jesus, Immanuel, is with me. Nothing can separate me from His love (Romans 8:37–39).

When life tosses me up in the air, I trust that I will be caught by my heavenly Father. I can know with certainty that God's purposes are being accomplished and that in some way He will make good come from whatever is happening (Romans 8:28 again). Finally, someday I will be carried in the arms of Jesus into heaven.

When life tosses me up in the air, I trust that I will be caught by my heavenly Father. I can know with certainty that God's purposes are being accomplished and that in some way He will make good come from whatever is happening (Romans 8:28 again). Finally, someday I will be carried in the arms of Jesus into heaven.

I was a mother of two sons and a classroom teacher for many years when the magnitude of God's love hit me in an unexpected way. At the time, the national news was filled with survivor ac-

counts of a horrific school shooting. The events had everyone thinking about school security. I wondered, "What would I do if a gunman entered my classroom while I taught?" I looked at my students and examined my heart. I loved them. I knew their parents. I thought, "I could give up my life for them." That year one of my own sons sat in my classroom. In moment of perfect clarity, I knew that while I might give my own life for my students, I would not willingly give my son's life for them. Immediately the words of John 3:16 came to mind: "For God so loved the world, that He gave His only Son."

In verse 10, this wonderful psalm, Psalm 32, nears its end with a creedal statement of David's faith in a God whose love never fails, a God whose love was proven beyond doubt by the giving of His Son!

But steadfast love surrounds the one who trusts in the Lord.

David knew of God's unfailing love. He experienced it. The final lines of this psalm speak of rejoicing. To rejoice is to be filled with joy, delighted! One of my children used to sing at the dinner table. It usually happened when the day had been good, the meal served was warm and delicious, and the family was together. A deep humming seemed to just pour out of his little body while he ate. I smile as I remember those moments. His delight was obvious, and his joy was both emotional and physical. That's how I imagine heaven to be. I hope you'll be there with me, with Mom and Dad, Aunt Ruth and Uncle Les, with Jack and my other siblings, and all our brothers and sisters in Christ. That certainly sounds delightful to me! Who's that singing at the table? Oh yeah—everyone!

Be glad in the Lord, and rejoice,
O righteous, and shout for joy, all you upright in heart!
Psalm 32:11

Prayer: Dear heavenly Father, never let me forget that I am safe in the arms of Your love. Although I am tossed up and down by life's many challenges, You have caught me forever in Jesus. Through His precious blood, cleanse me of my sins and renew my childlike faith. In Jesus' name. Amen.

Friday

Personal Study Questions: Psalm 32:10–11

1. In what ways do you belong to those labeled "wicked" in verse 10?

2. You also belong to those the text calls "righteous" (v. 11). How can that be true?

3. When have you experienced the overwhelming joy described in verse 11? How is the joy of sins forgiven truly essential, a prerequisite as it were, to experiencing any other true joy—here on earth or in heaven?

Group Bible Study for Week Five
Psalm 32

1. How does Psalm 32 fit in with the other psalms in the volume that you have explored under the theme "All of Your Wonderful Deeds"?

2. What key insights or fresh perspectives have you gained from your study of this week's faith narratives and the text of Psalm 32?

3. Time and again, highly placed government officials and leaders in the private sector, too, are caught in one kind of cover-up or another.

   a. Why does this tend to happen, even when the perpetrators are almost certain to be caught and prosecuted?

   b. When do you face the temptation to cover up your sins rather than confessing them?

   c. When we cover up our own sins, what happens (vv. 3–4)?

   d. When we uncover our sins, confessing them to God and in repentance and faith asking His forgiveness, what happens (vv. 5, 11)?

4. Compare the opening verses of this penitential psalm with the opening verses of two or three other psalms usually thought to belong to this category (Psalms 38; 51; 102; 130; and 143).

  a. What differences do you notice?

  b. What could account for these differences?

  c. When might you use Psalm 32 in your own devotional time as you seek to grow closer to your Lord?

5. If you were to write your own faith narrative based on a verse or several verses, which verses would you choose and what might you write about? Share with group members as you can do so comfortably.

Psalm 106

¹ Praise the LORD!
Oh give thanks to the LORD, for He is good,
for His steadfast love endures forever!

² Who can utter the mighty deeds of the LORD,
or declare all His praise?

³ Blessed are they who observe justice,
who do righteousness at all times!

⁴ Remember me, O LORD, when You show favor
to Your people;
help me when You save them,

⁵ that I may look upon the prosperity of Your
chosen ones,
that I may rejoice in the gladness of Your nation,
that I may glory with Your inheritance.

⁶ Both we and our fathers have sinned;
we have committed iniquity; we have done
wickedness.

⁷ Our fathers, when they were in Egypt,
did not consider Your wondrous works;
they did not remember the abundance of Your
steadfast love,
but rebelled by the sea, at the Red Sea.

⁸ Yet He saved them for His name's sake,
that He might make known His mighty power.

⁹ He rebuked the Red Sea, and it became dry,
and He led them through the deep as through a
desert.

¹⁰ So He saved them from the hand of the foe
and redeemed them from the power of the enemy.

¹¹ And the waters covered their adversaries;
not one of them was left.

¹² Then they believed His words;
they sang His praise.

¹³ But they soon forgot His works;
they did not wait for His counsel.

¹⁴ But they had a wanton craving in the wilderness,
and put God to the test in the desert;

¹⁵ He gave them what they asked,
but sent a wasting disease among them.

¹⁶ When men in the camp were jealous of Moses
and Aaron, the holy one of the LORD,

¹⁷ the earth opened and swallowed up Dathan,
and covered the company of Abiram.

¹⁸ Fire also broke out in their company;
the flame burned up the wicked.

¹⁹ They made a calf in Horeb
and worshiped a metal image.

²⁰ They exchanged the glory of God
for the image of an ox that eats grass.

²¹ They forgot God, their Savior,
who had done great things in Egypt,

²² wondrous works in the land of Ham,
and awesome deeds by the Red Sea.

²³ Therefore He said He would destroy them—
had not Moses, His chosen one,
stood in the breach before Him,
to turn away His wrath from destroying them.

²⁴ Then they despised the pleasant land,
having no faith in His promise.

²⁵ They murmured in their tents,
and did not obey the voice of the LORD.

²⁶ Therefore He raised His hand and swore to them
that He would make them fall in the wilderness,

²⁷ and would make their offspring fall among the nations,
scattering them among the lands.

²⁸ Then they yoked themselves to the Baal of Peor,
and ate sacrifices offered to the dead;

²⁹ they provoked the LORD to anger with their deeds,
and a plague broke out among them.

³⁰ Then Phinehas stood up and intervened,
and the plague was stayed.

³¹ And that was counted to him as righteousness
from generation to generation forever.

³² They angered Him at the waters of Meribah,
and it went ill with Moses on their account,

³³ for they made his spirit bitter,
and he spoke rashly with his lips.

³⁴ They did not destroy the peoples,
as the LORD commanded them,

³⁵ but they mixed with the nations
and learned to do as they did.

³⁶ They served their idols,
which became a snare to them.

³⁷ They sacrificed their sons
and their daughters to the demons;

³⁸ they poured out innocent blood,

the blood of their sons and daughters,
whom they sacrificed to the idols of Canaan,
and the land was polluted with blood.

³⁹ Thus they became unclean by their acts,
and played the whore in their deeds.

⁴⁰ Then the anger of the LORD was kindled against His people,
and He abhorred His heritage;

⁴¹ He gave them into the hand of the nations,
so that those who hated them ruled over them.

⁴² Their enemies oppressed them,
and they were brought into subjection under their power.

⁴³ Many times He delivered them,
but they were rebellious in their purposes
and were brought low through their iniquity.

⁴⁴ Nevertheless, He looked upon their distress,
when He heard their cry.

⁴⁵ For their sake He remembered His covenant,
and relented according to the abundance of His steadfast love.

⁴⁶ He caused them to be pitied
by all those who held them captive.

⁴⁷ Save us, O LORD our God,
and gather us from among the nations,
that we may give thanks to Your holy name
and glory in Your praise.

⁴⁸ Blessed be the LORD, the God of Israel,
from everlasting to everlasting!
And let all the people say, "Amen!"
Praise the LORD!

Eva Rickman

Psalm 106:1–12

Praise the LORD! Oh give thanks to the LORD, for He is good, for His steadfast love endures forever!

Praise the Lord!

I remember moving into my dorm at California State University, Long Beach, the weekend before classes started. It was an adventure; the first time I would truly be out on my own! Of course, I also had a lot of mixed emotions about leaving home, especially since my mom was battling cancer. But more than anything, I remember craving the freedom dorm life would bring. I no longer had to give an account to my parents about where I was going, how long I would be gone, or what time I would be home.

Still, rules were issued by the university and enforced by the RAs (residential assistants), but as anyone who has experienced dorm life knows, those rules are almost always broken. Consciences dull and temptations abound. Within the first week, our suite already had a pet, various young men had spent the night, empty beer cans appeared in the trash can of our common room, our neighbors regularly smoked outside our window on the stairwell (and not just cigarettes), and all of us were guilty of lighting candles or incense in our rooms.

I must admit my roommate, Brianna, and I were very naïve. We were both raised in families with similar values, and we grew up in the same church. We knew the difference between right and wrong, but more often than not, we became more and more comfortable with the behavior of our suitemates. The first few weeks of college, we had late-night conversations about how we could set a good example for them, but who were we kidding? One of the girls was the daughter of a pastor, they all had parents, and they didn't need us to tell them what to do.

Just as the Israelites rebelled against God (Psalm 106:7), my suitemates rebelled against their parents and university authorities. Even I went through periods of rebellion. I joined four different campus ministry groups, attended different churches on the weekends with my friends, and rebelled against organized religion and the worship of my youth. While a few of these campus ministries did indeed strengthen my faith, the majority of them made me question it. Was I Lutheran solely because I was born into it? Did I really have faith if I couldn't feel God working in my life? Why didn't I have an exact moment in my life when I made a decision for Christ? Was my Baptism valid if I was baptized as a baby? If I had enough faith, would God heal my mom who was dying from cancer? Is it really possible to praise God in a traditional worship service? All these questions and others danced around my mind as I rebelled more and more against the beliefs I was raised with.

The opening verse of Psalm 106 reads, "Praise the Lord! Oh give thanks to the Lord, for He is good, for His steadfast love endures forever!" Throughout my first year of college, I thought I was doing just that—praising the Lord. After all, I was attending weekly praise nights for each of the campus ministries I was involved in, as well as a special worship service every Sunday night on the campus of a local Christian university.

After nearly a year of attending these services and focusing on what I could do to be a better person, I finally realized what was missing. The services I attended catered to my emotions. They focused primarily on living a Christian life with Christ as our example. Throughout that year I kept looking for the next emotional and spiritual high, but I was never truly satisfied. Do you know why? The speakers kept telling me I was a good person and with God's help I could be even better. I felt more and more like a hypocrite because there was no talk about my sinfulness, only how I could overcome it. Little by little I was dying inside. No matter how hard I tried, I knew I could not be perfect.

God is faithful, He keeps His promises to us, and even when "we are faithless, He remains faithful—for He cannot deny Himself" (2 Timothy 2:13). In Christ, God has saved us from each and every sin we commit.

Yet perfection in this life is what these groups demanded; they convinced me that God demanded me to be perfect. God does indeed demand our perfection, but they were leaving out the part about how none of us is righteous (Romans 3:10), none of us "do[es] righteousness at all times!" (Psalm 106:3), and that is the reason we need Jesus. If there is never a chance to confess our sins, how can we be absolved of them? I was left without hope because I heard nothing about our precious Savior, Jesus Christ, only about what I needed to do to be a better Christian.

But since I "have sinned," "have committed iniquity," and "have done wickedness," I now cry to the Lord with the psalmist: "Remember me, O LORD, when You show favor to Your people; help me when You save them" (v. 4). And you know what? God does just that! God is faithful, He keeps His promises to us, and even when "we are faithless, He remains faithful—for He cannot deny Himself" (2 Timothy 2:13). In Christ, God has saved us from each and every sin we commit. I eventually learned that praising God is neither me having an emotional experience nor me focusing on what I could do for God. Rather, praising God is extolling what He has already done for me in my Savior. My heavenly Father sent Jesus, His only Son, to die on my behalf, and through His death and resurrection I have eternal life.

Since my first year in college, I have grown to love the richness and the depth of the liturgy. We enter the sanctuary from a world full of sin, not pretending to be perfect people (1 John 1:8). Instead, we confess our sinfulness and our great need for Christ's mercy. In turn, we receive His mercy and pardon as the pastor proclaims to us in the stead of Christ that our sins indeed are forgiven! It is that mercy and that forgiveness that leads me to "praise the LORD!"

Like the Israelites, we do not think of God's miracles or remember His mercy; instead, we continue to rebel in our daily lives. Yet as God delivered Israel through the waters of the Red Sea, daily through the waters of our Baptism, we have God's promise that we are His daughters, "buried therefore with Him by baptism into death, in order that, just as Christ was raised from the dead by the glory of the Father, we too might walk in newness of life" (Romans 6:4). My Baptism as an infant was valid, indeed, because God's promise does not depend on the faith I had as an infant but on His Word and promise given through the waters of Baptism.

Naturally, we praise God for our families and friends and how He provides us with food and a place to live. But even more, we praise God because He leads, saves, and redeems us just as He led, saved, and redeemed the Israelites. His promises were true for them, and they are true for us as well. We can rejoice in God's promises, "utter[ing] the mighty deeds of the LORD" (v. 2) with all those who have used the Psalms to "praise the LORD!"

Eva

Prayer: Heavenly Father, I have sinned against You and my neighbors. Yet You redeemed me through the precious blood of Jesus, Your only Son. By Your Holy Spirit, strengthen my faith always to believe in Your promises and sing Your praises. In Jesus' name. **Amen.**

Eva

monday

Personal Study Questions:
Psalm 106:1–12

The psalmist begins Psalm 106 by exclaiming, "Oh give thanks to the LORD for *He* is good" (emphasis added). Then he goes on to contrast the Lord's goodness with the behavior of God's people over many centuries—behavior we might describe as anything but good! As we read the psalm, we find ourselves, too, saying "*He* is good, not I."

1. What specific evidence of "not goodness" does the psalmist give as he thinks of his ancestry—ancient Israel? With what specific evidence of the Lord's goodness does he contrast Israel's sinfulness?

2. What specific evidence of her own "not goodness" does the author of today's faith narrative cite? With what specific evidence of the Lord's goodness does she contrast her own sinfulness?

3. What specific evidence of your own "not goodness" can you cite? What specific evidence of the Lord's continuing goodness and love can you cite in contrast?

Eva

Psalm 106:13–23

They exchanged the glory of God for the image of an ox that eats grass. They forgot God, their Savior, who had done great things in Egypt, wondrous works in the land of Ham, and awesome deeds by the Red Sea.

Got Idols?

Idol worship was never more apparent to me than in India, where I visited a Hindu temple. After the people in my group and I took off our shoes and the men removed their shirts, we entered the temple. I was instantly absorbed in all the unfamiliar sights, sounds, and smells around me.

As we walked clockwise through the temple, we encountered altars, which were devoted to various animal gods. Loud drums, bells, and clouds of incense captured my senses. At the various altars, I observed people worshiping these idols—their gods. One woman

Eva

184

was decorating a statue of Hanuman, the monkey god, with a wreath of flowers, while a Hindu monk, dressed only in an orange skirt, was kneeling and bowing down before Ganesha, the Hindu deity with an elephant head and a human body. Other worshipers brought offerings of fruit or flowers. I saw one older woman weeping as she offered a prayer to another animal deity. I remember my heart pounding to the beat of the drums. I felt like I had just walked into the pages of the Scriptures where the Israelites worshiped the golden calf at the base of Mount Sinai (Exodus 32). As we were led into the center pavilion where a ceremony was taking place, I remember praying for these people who trusted in idols instead of in the one, true, living, triune God.

As a Christian, you may be thinking you would never be led astray and get caught up in crass idol worship, like what I have described here. After all, you are familiar with the Ten Commandments, where in the very first commandment God forbids us to have any other gods besides Him (Exodus 20:3–6). As Christians, it is easy for us to identify worship like what I observed in India as idol worship. In addition to the specific idols I've mentioned, there were others devoted to elephants, cows, and so on. Hindu monks and temple visitors brought offerings to these idols, bowing down in prayer to the various images of their gods.

You know, as Christians it is easy to criticize Hindu worship and put ourselves on a pedestal by thinking that we would never worship idols. But do we?

You are probably familiar with the television show *American Idol*, in which people from all over the country compete for fame and fortune as the next popular American singer. What exactly is an idol? Like the idols I observed in the Hindu temple, an idol certainly can be an image of a god or deity people use as the object of their worship. However, an idol can also be defined as anything or anyone that consumes us and distracts us from worshiping the one, true God. Furthermore, Ephesians 5:5 clearly shows us that anyone who is covetous, whether it be for fame or fortune, is an idolater.

Even as a Christian, I am guilty of having idols in my life, and you probably are too. I admit that I constantly get distracted by the world around me. I forget what God has done and do not wait for His counsel (v. 13). While I do not have a statue of a golden calf sitting in the living room of our apartment (and I hope you don't either), I have my own idols sculpted out of the clay of my own desires, chiseled from the stone of my sinfulness, carved from my wooden pride, and cast from the gold of my greed. There are many things in my life that daily distract me from God as I compare my life to the lives of those around me. Our houses, cars, televisions, computers, money, and other possessions all can become idols that slowly push God out of our lives. Sports, careers, other people, and even we ourselves can become our idols as we strive for the perfect body, wear the most fashionable clothes, and obsess about the way we appear to others.

> *With Christ before us as an even greater Moses, we can walk out of the darkness, casting aside the idols that divert our attention from God, and enter into the light of Christ. Jesus alone is our advocate, and He stands before the Father, pointing to the cross where He died so we can live.*

Even our time can become an idol. As the Israelites "forgot God, their Savior" (v. 21), so we, too, forget our Lord and Savior as our days become filled with one more meeting, one more after-school activity, one more video game, and so on. Our jobs, our families, and our material possessions all slowly cause us to push God aside and trade Him in for these idols that slowly consume us. Like the Israelites "exchanged the glory of God for the image of an ox that eats grass" (v. 20), so we, too, in our daily lives trade the things of God for the things in this world. In an age of self-help books and workshops geared at getting to know ourselves better, people rely less and less on God as they cling more and more to the promises of the world. But the world deceives us and makes us think that we can have the perfect job, the perfect house, the perfect family, and the perfect life if only we trust in ourselves and work a little harder.

Sorry to break it to you, but the promises of this world and the idols in our lives only distract us from what is really important—the promises of God. As the idols in our lives hold

us captive and lure us away from God, the Gospel frees us from the bondage of sin. Not only do the idols in our lives distract us, but they actually destroy us, bring God's wrath on us when we are disobedient, and keep us from inheriting the kingdom of God (Ephesians 5:5–6). We are all guilty of forgetting God, our Savior, who led the Israelites out of Egypt, and we are all guilty of trusting in the idols in our lives above the living God (v. 21).

For our unfaithfulness, we deserve to be destroyed by God's wrath, but as "Moses, His chosen one, stood in the breach before Him, to turn away His wrath from destroying them" (v. 23), so Christ, our Savior, keeps His wrath from us. With Christ before us as an even greater Moses, we can walk out of the darkness, casting aside the idols that divert our attention from God, and enter into the light of Christ. Jesus alone is our advocate, and He stands before the Father, pointing to the cross where He died so we can live. "But He was wounded for our transgressions; He was crushed for our iniquities; upon Him was the chastisement that brought us peace, and with His stripes we are healed" (Isaiah 53:5). Now, no idol can do that!

Prayer: Dear Lord, I confess to You that I have allowed idols to consume my life instead of focusing on You and Your promises. Help me to turn away from them and put my trust in You alone. Thank You for sending Jesus to redeem me from my sins so I may enter Your kingdom. In Jesus' name I pray. Amen.

Eva

tuesday

Personal Study Questions: Psalm 106:13–23

1. What constitutes an idol, a false god?

2. Today's faith narrative notes that you probably don't have a golden statue of a false god in your living room to which you kneel in prayer. But what false gods regularly receive your highest "fear, love, and trust"?

3. Despite the seriousness of Israel's sin, Moses stepped in as an intercessor, and God averted His wrath (v. 23).

a. How does Moses' action picture and foreshadow the ministry of our Lord Jesus?

b. When did Jesus stand "in the breach" for you?
(See Hebrews 10:19–22.)

Psalm 106:24–33

Then they despised the pleasant land, having no faith in His promise. They murmured in their tents, and did not obey the voice of the LORD.

Always Wanting Something More

As a child, I remember being so excited about growing up. Each year, I couldn't wait for another birthday so I could be one year older and one year closer to being a grown-up. You see, I thought that by being a grown-up I wouldn't have to follow any rules: I could go to bed late and eat whatever I wanted for dinner (I certainly would have chosen mint chip ice cream). And each year as I

Eva

189

turned a year older, I was excited by the new privileges that came along with my new age. But my contentment in that new age didn't last long. Usually a week or two later, I would find myself disappointed again because I still couldn't do everything I wanted to do or everything my older sister could do. Each year, I thought I would finally catch up to her, but soon I realized that each time I added another year to my age, in another two months, she would add another year to her age as well.

We don't have to go around grumbling about what we do not have because God daily provides for our needs. It is in the pure grace of God alone through faith in Christ that we have hope, yet even this faith is not of ourselves but is a gift of the Holy Spirit.

Let me tell you, my discontentment didn't end when I reached adulthood either, although I recall at least one night when I did have mint chip ice cream for dinner. As I entered college, the murmurings of discontent followed me as I soon realized that it wasn't so easy to go to college and work to be able to pay for tuition and housing. At that point, childhood didn't seem to be so bad after all. But since I knew I couldn't go back, I looked ahead to graduation when I could get married and start a life with my husband, only to wish I was back in school a few months after graduation. Then, when that wish came true as my husband and I moved to St. Louis to study at the seminary, we were again longing for full-time jobs that would help us pay our tuition and basic living expenses. At the same time, we couldn't wait to start serving in the mission field.

No matter what, I was never satisfied and always wanted something more as I continually focused on the goals, grumbling along the way instead of enjoying the journey.

Our lives are so filled with anticipation for what is coming that we often fail to appreciate and sometimes even despise the blessings God gives us. Now you may be thinking that sounds a little harsh and that you have never despised the blessings of God, but that is exactly what we do when doubts creep into our thoughts and we lack faith in God's promises. We are like the Israelites in Psalm 106:24–25, who "despised the pleasant land, having no faith in His promise. They murmured in their tents,

Eva

and did not obey the voice of the LORD." How often do we do the same? How many times would we rather grumble to our friends about our jobs, our families, and even God instead of trusting in His promises?

The Bible is full of examples of unbelief. Adam and Eve certainly didn't trust the Creator's promise when they were biting into that juicy fruit (Genesis 3:6); Zechariah questioned the angel Gabriel who proclaimed that his wife would give birth to John the Baptist (Luke 1:18); and Sarah laughed at the Lord's promise that she would give birth in her old age (Genesis 18:12). Furthermore, the Israelites were constantly grumbling and complaining to the Lord even to the point where they longed for Egypt, the place of their bondage, over the Promised Land. Can you believe that they would long for captivity over the land flowing with milk and honey?

Looking into the Scriptures and reading the account of the Israelites, it is easy to see their unbelief. It is also easy to see how they missed God's promises because they were too focused on themselves. How often are we in the same situation, grumbling about the struggles in our lives and failing to praise the Lord for our daily blessings? When we murmur against God, our ears become so full of our words that it is hard to hear God. We indulge in our own words of disbelief, which keep us wandering in the desert instead of praising God in the Promised Land.

St. Paul tells us, "Do all things without grumbling or questioning, that you may be blameless and innocent, children of God without blemish in the midst of a crooked and twisted generation, among whom you shine as lights in the world, holding fast to the word of life, so that in the day of Christ I may be proud that I did not run in vain or labor in vain" (Philippians 2:14–16).

I don't know about you, but I would much rather shine like the stars in the heavens than be caught up in murmurings that distract us from God. I certainly do not want to be guilty of having "provoked the LORD to anger" like the Israelites did (v. 29). Still, I know I constantly fail and deserve nothing but God's wrath.

Eva

But, dear sisters, do not lose hope! The Lord's promise to Paul rings true for us as well:

But He said to me, "My grace is sufficient for you, for My power is made perfect in weakness." Therefore I will boast all the more gladly of my weaknesses, so that the power of Christ may rest upon me. For the sake of Christ, then, I am content with weaknesses, insults, hardships, persecutions, and calamities. For when I am weak, then I am strong.
2 Corinthians 12:9–10

Did you catch that? God's grace is sufficient! We don't have to go around grumbling about what we do not have because God daily provides for our needs. It is in the pure grace of God alone through faith in Christ that we have hope, yet even this faith is not of ourselves but is a gift of the Holy Spirit, who works faith in us (Ephesians 2:8–9). And it is Christ alone, our manna, the "bread that came down from heaven," who gives us life (John 6:41). Christ offers us so much more than the manna sent to the Israelites, for they ate the manna and died, but we partake of the body and blood of Christ and live forever (John 6:58).

What more could we want? Not only does Christ promise us eternal life at His holy Table, but He also promises to raise us up on the Last Day (John 6:54). And He doesn't stop there! He forgives each and every one of our sins and even our grumblings.

Indeed, what more could we want?

Prayer: Dear Lord, please forgive my grumblings and my lack of trust in Your unfailing promises. Thank You for sending Jesus, my living bread, to nourish me and to give me eternal life. Help me to not be so focused on the past and present that I lose sight of Your eternal promises. In Jesus' name I pray. **Amen.**

Eva

wednesday

Personal Study Questions: Psalm 106:24–33

1. When are you most likely to be overheard by your Lord "murmuring in your tent" like the Israelites did in verse 25? From what deeper, additional sin does your complaining most often spring?

2. How does the author's use of 2 Corinthians 12:9–10 in today's faith narrative and her remarks associated with this passage bring you comfort and hope?

Eva

Psalm 106:34–43

They did not destroy the peoples, as the LORD commanded them, but they mixed with the nations and learned to do as they did. They served their idols, which became a snare to them. They sacrificed their sons and their daughters to the demons.

Mixing with the Nations

As a deaconess serving in the mission field of Latin America, I observe almost daily the mingling of nations, cultures, customs, and religions. Last year, I attended a language school in Guatemala. My Spanish teacher, Dora, opened my eyes to the various pagan rituals still performed by people who claim to be Christian. To give you a little background, Dora is the most devout person I have ever met. On most days, she attended services both in the morning and in the evening. She always at-

Eva

194

tended Sunday worship, and when we would walk around town to practice Spanish, she would pay her respects each time we passed a church. She even told me that as a young girl, she always wanted to serve the church but decided against it because she wanted to get married and have a family. All her actions indicated to me that she was committed to her faith.

After several months of intense language study, I was finally at the point where I could start asking more questions about her faith, and she openly shared with me. In one conversation, she told me about going to Chichicastenango with her husband. There they could visit a church and light candles for their ancestors and for the king who was buried in the Mayan temple lying under the church. At first, I was confused and unsure if I understood her Spanish correctly. After all, she was a devout Christian, so why would she be worshiping her ancestors and this Mayan king? To my surprise, she repeated herself and confirmed what she had told me. I later found out that Santo Tomas, the cathedral in Chichicastenango, was only one of several churches in Guatemala where Mayan rituals took place side by side with Christian ones.

Another day, she took me to see an altar to the deity Maximón (Mah-shee-mon). I thought she was taking me there as an American so I could learn more about the history and culture of Guatemala. However, as we approached the altar with a figure of a seated man wearing a hat and smoking a cigar, I observed her kneeling in front of the altar and lighting a candle to this deity that was surrounded with offerings of flowers, rum, and candles. She later told me that she was asking for his blessing. Over the next several months, she told me stories about how eclipses cause pregnant women to give birth to deformed babies and how her family called a shaman to take away the evil spirits that were causing her brother's illness. Dora is only one of many Guatemalans who identify themselves as Christians yet still hold firmly to many of the rituals of traditional Mayan worship. (In the past, the Mayans were even known for human sacrifices.)

Like the Israelites, many churches in Guatemala "mixed with the nations and learned to do as they did. They served their

Eva

idols, which became a snare to them. They sacrificed their sons and their daughters to the demons" (vv. 35–37) as they held firmly to their pagan rituals under the veil of Christianity.

In the United States, the melting pot of the world, we are not immune to this mixing of nations. American society often influences Christian churches more than our churches influence society. Maybe we don't have altars to Maximón, but if we look close enough, we can see the subtle ways the Church has "mixed with the nations and learned to do as they did" (v. 35).

The Holy Spirit helps us to overcome cultural pitfalls. In Christ, we may be despised for choosing the path of righteousness, but we can never be snatched out of the Father's hands. The Lord will provide strength the moment we need it.

How many times have we watched movies and television shows with steamy sex scenes or listened to music with foul language without even batting an eye? Are these just "entertainment," or are we mixing with the culture and adopting worldly standards of right and wrong? These things can often become "a snare" without our even realizing it (v. 36). They creep into our lives undetected because they are commonplace and acceptable in our culture (v. 36). We become desensitized. In our daily lives, we conform our personal values to current cultural values—how we spend our time, what is foremost in our thoughts, how we speak or behave, what we stand for or what we stand up to, the ambitions that drive us. Are you mixing with the nations?

In verse 37, the psalmist talks about the Israelites sacrificing their sons and daughters to demons. American culture doesn't condone child sacrifices. But do we sacrifice our children's Christian values when we let them watch inappropriate shows and listen to harmful music? Are we condoning such behavior instead of training them up in the way they should go (Proverbs 22:6)? And in our culture, there has been a whole generation of preborn babies who were sacrificed. How do we reconcile that fact with our Christianity?

Like the Israelites, we waste away in our sin (Psalm 106:14–15). We fail to confess Christ, and we constantly mingle with those things that lead us astray from His promises. Just as God

handed the Israelites over to their enemies who oppressed them, there are consequences to our actions as well (vv. 41–42). By our own sinfulness, we disqualify ourselves from being God's chosen people. However, He does not give up on us. Like a loving father concerned about his children, He shows us where we have gone against His will as recorded in His Word. He reveals the consequences for our actions, and He leads us to repentance.

In His precious Gospel, God proclaims to us the sacrificial gift of His one and only Son, who died on the cross so we might live. Jesus' blood has set us free to be God's people. Daily through the promise we received in our Baptism, God forgives us and renews us as His new creation, cleansing us from each and every sin. Indeed, Baptism connects us to Jesus' death and resurrection: "We were buried therefore with Him by baptism into death, in order that, just as Christ was raised from the dead by the glory of the Father, we too might walk in newness of life" (Romans 6:4).

The one who transcends culture, who teaches us to live in the world and yet not be of the world, is Christ Jesus. Romans 6:11 says, "Consider yourselves dead to sin and alive to God in Christ Jesus." The Holy Spirit helps us to overcome cultural pitfalls. In Christ, we may be despised for choosing the path of righteousness, but we can never be snatched out of the Father's hands. The Lord will provide strength the moment we need it. Although they might mock the Lord and His Anointed One, He who is over all things cannot be defeated (Psalm 2:2). Through Him, neither can those who struggle with marriages in crisis or children who hear and see messages of hate, sex, and violence. In Christ, we have the promise that He has overcome the things of this world, and He is greater than Satan, who puts many snares before us. Therefore, dear sister, do not despair. The nations will not win because He who has claimed you has promised you that all that is of Christ is yours (1 Corinthians 3:21–23).

Eva

Prayer: Dear Lord, please forgive me for mixing with the nations and being distracted by the culture around me. Please strengthen me through Your Word to know Your will and what is pleasing to You. Help me to not be afraid to bear witness to Your mercy. In Jesus' name. **Amen.**

Eva

thursday

Personal Study Questions: Psalm 106:34–43

1. Verses 34–43 mince no words as they describe the sins of God's people. Where do you see yourself in this litany of idolatry and its consequences?

2. When have your sins oppressed and subjugated you? (See v. 42.) When has your iniquity "brought [you] low"? (See v. 43.)

3. Look ahead in the psalm to God's great "nevertheless"—in verse 44. How does that "nevertheless," activated by Christ on Calvary, stir hope in your heart despite your sins? How does your Baptism personalize that hope?

Eva

Psalm 106:44–48

Nevertheless, He looked upon their distress, when He heard their cry. For their sake He remembered His covenant, and relented according to the abundance of His steadfast love.

Tears Turned to Praise

Have you ever cried to the Lord? Have you ever been so overcome by fear, pain, or other heavy burdens that there was nothing you could do but cry to the Lord?

The first time I remember really crying to God was the summer before my high school senior year, when my mom was diagnosed with cancer. The day my parents told me about the diagnosis, I instantly felt like my world was crashing down around me. It was a shock that completely

Eva

200

overwhelmed me. No one else in our family had cancer. However, the previous year I had experienced the disease for the first time as both a classmate and my chemistry teacher died from cancer. This made me even more afraid of the disease, and now it had attacked one of the people I was closest to: my own mom. That night, I remember crying to the Lord—questioning, begging, and pleading.

During the next few years, I cried even more. Each time my mom would go in for more tests, another blood transfusion, another surgery, another round of radiation or chemo, I would cry. Each time we learned that the cancer had spread to her bones, her lungs, her brain, I cried even more. Cancer took a toll on our whole family and changed our lives in so many ways. Throughout those years, I was unable to turn to my family because they were all hurting just as much as I. Nor was I able to turn to my high school or college friends, whose biggest problems at the time revolved around which guy to date. Only in the Lord could I find strength. Just as He listened to the Israelites and "looked upon their distress, when He heard their cry" (v. 44), I know He heard my cries as well.

My mom was very involved in our church and school activities and volunteered a lot of her time. She had many friends and was always willing to help others. That is why so many people, when they learned she had cancer, remarked how she was such a good person and that it was a shame she had to suffer. My mom indeed was a good person who devoted her life to her family and sacrificed her career to raise my sister and me. But like all of us, she, too, was sinful. Romans 3:23 clearly reveals that "all have sinned and fall short of the glory of God."

Many times people try to justify why bad things happen. People accept that bad people are punished for the evil they do but find it hard to understand why good people like my mom suffer. After all, she didn't do anything to warrant such pain. Granted, the individual sins of my mom did not lead to her battle with cancer. But cancer, AIDS, leukemia, and all diseases can lead to death and, indeed, all are the result of sin. Since Adam and

Eva

Eve's fall in the Garden of Eden, we have lived in a world tainted by sin that leads only to death. Sin comes with a hefty penalty, consequences that we have had to live with since Adam and Eve disobeyed our heavenly Father. The Scriptures are clear that the "wages of sin is death" (Romans 6:23) and that death is the end that awaits us all no matter how good we are.

God is faithful to us through the covenant of His Son's blood shed for us on the cross. My cries have turned into praise because I have faith that my mom is in paradise with Christ, awaiting the resurrection.

Specific sins often come with consequences as well. Premarital sex can result in an unplanned pregnancy, and drunk drivers can injure or kill innocent people. The Israelites experienced consequences for their sins. For their rebellion, worshiping idols, and failing to trust in and praise God, the Israelites suffered many consequences, including being handed over to their oppressive enemies. But God "heard their cry" and "remembered His covenant" (vv. 44–45) just as God remembers His promises to us in our Baptism (Mark 16:16). Dear sister, remember Romans 6:23? It doesn't end with death. Sure "the wages of sin is death," but hear the precious Gospel: "the free gift of God is eternal life in Christ Jesus our Lord." If God can remember the covenant He had with the Israelites and forgive all their rebellions, He certainly can forgive each and every one of our sins. He remembers His covenant with us through the blood of Christ (1 Corinthians 11:25). What a blessing to know that we can continue our lives as redeemed children of God living under the cross of Christ!

God is merciful and, for Christ's sake, forgives us completely. Still, we continue to live with the consequences of sin, both our sins and the sins of others. Just as the Lord did not free the Israelites from captivity, God does not promise to take away the consequences of our sins. Nevertheless, just as He caused the Israelites "to be pitied by all those who held them captive," God can cause others around us to have pity on us, making the consequences of our sins more bearable (v. 46). What a wonderful God we have! Can you believe that God can even change the hearts of our enemies and cause them to have compassion on us? Not only does He grant us the spiritual blessings of eternal life through

Eva

Christ, but He also has pity on us and can change the hearts of those who oppress us.

Remember, dear sister, the Lord is merciful, and the weight of heartache over a sin confessed and forgiven is not the Lord judging you but Satan looking to make you, a daughter of the heavenly Father, fall into despair. Satan tries to convince us that our sins are so grievous that God is still punishing us. But take heart! It is not so. He will not forget His promises to you because He is faithful. When you feel burdened, you can call upon Him and He will deliver you—you are forgiven. He loves you so much that He even makes those around you, even your enemies, pity you. They do not pity you because you are pitiful but because God is merciful and shows you His mercy even through your enemies. Dear sister, do not despair, for Christ is with you and has promised that final victory—even over that weight you now bear—on that great and awesome resurrection day.

Psalm 106 begins and ends with praise because God is faithful to His covenant people. God is faithful to us through the covenant of His Son's blood shed for us on the cross. My cries have turned into praise because I have faith that my mom is in paradise with Christ, awaiting the resurrection. As we make the sign of the cross in remembrance of our Baptism, we are reminded that like our father and mother, Adam and Eve, we, too, will face death in this world as the result of our sins, but eternally we will live because Christ lives. God remembers His promises. What more can we do but praise the Lord for His wonderful deeds!

Eva

Prayer: "Save us, O LORD our God, and gather us from among the nations, that we may give thanks to Your holy name and glory in Your praise. Blessed be the LORD, the God of Israel, from everlasting to everlasting! And let all the people say, 'Amen!' Praise the LORD!" (Psalm 106:47–48).

Eva

Personal Study Questions:
Psalm 106:44–48

1. Think of a time when you literally cried out as you prayed during a time of deep distress (v. 44).

   a. How did it help to know that your Savior heard your words and saw your tears?

   b. How did it help to know that He remembered the covenant He made with you in Baptism?

   c. How did He show you His love by sending other people—even those you might not have expected—across your path to help you in answer to your prayers?

2. In what ways does verse 47 reflect the glories and the joy of heaven? In what ways does our Lord answer this prayer for His people even now, here on earth?

Eva

Group Bible Study for Week Six
Psalm 106

1. In what ways did the faith narratives from this week add to your understanding of Psalm 106? Give a few specific examples.

2. Psalm 106 walks the reader through what we might call a short history of God's people from the time of creation to the time of the judges. It summarizes centuries of experience, singling out examples of events that demonstrate the psalmist's main point: God's wonderful grace contrasted with His people's utter failure to trust and obey Him.

   Choose a partner, and have each partner pair select one of the items below. Research the background from the texts suggested, and prepare an answer to your question, based on the text. Then take turns reporting back to the whole group.

   a. How does Psalm 106:1–5 reflect God's glory in the creation and in the history of Abraham, Isaac, and Jacob and their families? (See Genesis 1–50, but in the interest of time, focus especially on Genesis 1; 8; and 17; see also Genesis 50:22–26.)

   b. How does Psalm 106:6–12 reflect God's amazing mercy in delivering Israel from slavery in Egypt, despite their unbelief? (See Exodus 1–40; in the interest of time, you may want to focus especially on Exodus 14 and 15.)

   c. How does Psalm 106:13–23 reflect God's judgment and grace during Israel's wilderness wanderings after the Exodus? (See Exodus 1–40; in the interest of time, you may want to focus especially on Exodus 16; 17; and 32.)

   d. How does Psalm 106:24–27 accent God's patient mercy toward His rebellious people during their wilderness wanderings after the Exodus? (See the Book of Numbers, but in the interest of time, focus especially on Numbers 13 and 14.)

e. How does Psalm 106:28–33 reflect Israel's rebellion and God's compassion as described in Numbers 20:1–13 and 25:1–13?

f. How does Psalm 106:34–43 reflect the history of idolatry and disobedience recorded in the Book of Judges? (See especially Judges 2:11–19.)

3. As we have just seen, Psalm 106 summarizes centuries of history during which the Lord remained faithful to His covenant people despite enormous provocation to totally annihilate them for their sin, rebellion, and unbelief.

a. What is the point of this history lesson? In other words, why does the psalmist invite his readers to take this trip down memory lane, past so many of God's wonderful deeds?

b. Where do you see our culture and perhaps even today's Church in the warnings this psalm offers?

c. Where do you see yourself in the psalm and its warnings? in the psalm and its promises and the hope God here offers?

4. Twice in Psalm 106, the Holy Spirit calls attention to the work done by intercessors (v. 23 and vv. 29–31).

a. How do Phinehas and Moses both foreshadow Jesus' work on our behalf? See Romans 8:33–34.

b. For whom do you intercede most regularly? How do you know your prayers are heard? See James 5:16.

5. What makes verse 48 a fitting conclusion to Psalm 106? to our study of the psalms celebrating God's wonderful deeds?

Small-Group Leader Guide

This guide will help guide you in discovering the truths of God's Word. It is not, however, exhaustive, nor is it designed to be read aloud during your session.

1. Before you begin, spend some time in prayer, asking God to strengthen your faith through a study of His Word. The Scriptures were written so that we might believe in Jesus Christ and have life in His name (John 20:31). Also, pray for participants by name.

2. Before your meeting, review the session material, read the Bible passages, and answer the questions in the spaces provided. Your familiarity with the session will give you confidence as you lead the group.

3. As a courtesy to participants, begin and end each session on time.

4. Have a Bible dictionary or similar resource handy to look up difficult or unfamiliar names, words, and places. Ask participants to help you in this task. Be sure that each participant has a Bible and a study guide.

5. Ask for volunteers to read introductory paragraphs and Bible passages. A simple "thank you" will encourage them to volunteer again.

6. See your role as a conversation facilitator rather than a lecturer. Don't be afraid to give participants time to answer questions. By name, thank each participant who answers; then invite other input. For example, you may say, "Thank you, Maggie. Would anyone else like to share?"

7. Now and then, summarize aloud what the group has learned by studying God's Word.

8. Remember that the questions provided are discussion starters. Allow participants to ask questions that relate to the session. However, keep discussions on track with the session.

9. Everyone is a learner! If you don't know the answer to a question, simply tell participants that you need time to look at more Scripture passages or to ask your pastor.

Week 1, Psalm 9

Personal Study Questions

Monday—Psalm 9:1–4

1. Answers will vary.
2. Answers will vary.
3. Answers will vary.

Tuesday—Psalm 9:5–8

1. David praises God for maintaining his just cause; ruling with righteous judgments; rebuking the nations that opposed him and threatened God's people; making the wicked perish; and removing even the memory of the enemy's existence. Answers concerning God's merciful "you haves" in our lives today will vary.

2. In Christ, God has reconciled us—and the whole world—to Himself. He does not count our trespasses against us. Because Christ "became sin" for us, we have now become "the righteousness of God." All this has come to us "in Christ." Baptized into Him, we are full heirs to what some have called the Great Exchange. We receive Christ's very own right standing with the Father, while Jesus bears our sin and its penalty.

3. Answers will vary.

Wednesday—Psalm 9:9–12

1. Answers will vary. Luther explains that the First Commandment requires us to "fear, love, and trust" in God above everything else. When we succumb to the craving for control, we fail to trust God's love and to believe that in everything He is at work for our good. See Romans 8:28.

2. Answers will vary.
3. Answers will vary.

Thursday—Psalm 9:13–16

1. Verse 12 states the truth in general terms—the Lord does not forget or ignore the cries of the afflicted. In verse 13, then, David acts on this promise, crying out in his own affliction, trusting God to hear and help. We can join

him in confident hope that God will hear and deliver us as well.

2. The "gates of death" contrast with the "gates of the daughter of Zion"—thus contrasting the death and hell we rightly deserve because of our sins with the position of access to God and membership in His family, His Church, we have received as a gift in the cross of our Savior.

3. Answers will vary.

Friday—Psalm 9:17–20

1. David cries for help in his affliction several times in verses 11–20. His enemies "hate" him; he stands at "the gates of death"; the "wicked" have hidden a net to entrap him. Other answers are possible.

2. Like David, we too live in the gap, so to speak, between the promised, total victory Jesus has already won for us and the full realization of that victory. We will one day enjoy the full fruits of our Savior's work on our behalf. But for now, like David, we rely on the power of the Holy Spirit to work in us the "I wills" of praise that grow from a heart that trusts our mighty Savior God. Despite current challenges and difficulties, we live in hope and act with courage, God working this response of determination in us.

3. Answers will vary.

Group Bible Study

1. Answers will vary.

2. Answers will vary. Evidence of David's turmoil might include his references to "affliction," the "gates of death," his "enemies," and "the wicked." Refer to Monday's question 2, Friday's question 1, and the answers provided in this guide as you discuss the interplay between emotions and faith.

As we seek to help friends caught in the feelings-faith paradox, we first will listen to their pain and fear, just as God listens to us—in empathy and compassion. We will want to acknowledge the seriousness of their challenges. We will probably avoid saying things like "I know just how you feel," because we do not; even if we have experienced a very similar set of circumstances, our friend does not have the same background nor the same support system upon which we rely. After listening carefully, we might gently guide our friend to the truths of God's Word. Certainly, we could pray together for peace and courage and then repeat these steps as often as necessary, remembering that our Lord never tires of listening to us and helping us.

3. Like David, we can decide to speak and act from our faith rather than from our fears. We can rely upon the truths the Holy Spirit reveals to us in Scripture rather than on what our senses seem to be telling us at any given moment.

4. The wicked and all the trouble they cause and the anxiety they create will soon fall into ruin. The righteous, those who belong to God in Christ, will not even remember then! The "cities" they build, the values they transmit, the victories they claim—all these will dissolve to dust and blow away. In contrast, our Savior-God, the Most High, the covenant-making, covenant-keeping Lord who has claimed us in our Baptism sits "enthroned forever"; His love, mercy, and goodness to us will never end! Sin and Satan, hell and death, sickness and persecution, pain and loss, loneliness and need, injustice and war will all one day come to an abrupt end. Jesus will rule in righteousness and grace in the new heaven and new earth. See Revelation 21:1–7.

5. Answers will vary. Let group members share insights.

6. Answers will vary.

7. Answers will vary.

Week 2, Psalm 18

Personal Study Questions

Monday—Psalm 18:1–12

1. David, though king by this time in his personal history, identifies himself instead as "the servant of the LORD." Saul and other troublesome, hate-filled enemies have fallen, judged and punished by the Righteous One; David has been vindicated. He sings the new hymn he has written in response to God's goodness.

2. Answers will vary. Our God is a personal God who takes a personal interest in each of us, His children. Better than being "Bernie's daughters," we belong to the Rock!

3. Answers will vary. Several words and phrases in Psalm 18 draw upon the imagery of thunder, lightning, wind, and an approaching storm front. The Lord was fiercely angry at David's enemies; His anger is described as sharp and fierce as lightning bolts. As quickly as a thunderstorm blows over the desert, so quickly, deliberately, and relentlessly the Savior-God came to His

people's rescue. God parted the waters of the Red Sea to rescue Israel from Pharaoh's army, drying out the seabed with a strong east wind. Similarly now, nothing will stop His drive to protect and deliver the psalmist—and us! (vv. 13–15). The fierce wind, the "blast" of the Lord's "breath," parted the waters, laying even the "channels of the sea" bare to open the way for Him to come to His people in His saving power (v. 15).

Tuesday—Psalm 18:13–19

    1. Answers will vary.

    2. Answers will vary.

    3. Answers will vary.

    4. The truth that God "delights" in us can be a "How?" if we forget Christ's sacrifice and begin to think we must earn God's pleasure by our own efforts. The truth that God "delights" in us can be a "Wow!" in that our sins should evoke only disgust in His heart, resulting in our dismissal from His presence. But because of our Savior, Jesus, and His cross, God now declares us blameless and holy. He loves us with a love unshakable!

Wednesday—Psalm 18:20–30

    1. David writes here about the right standing with God theologians sometimes call "imputed righteousness"—the righteousness that God freely gives to those who cling to Christ in repentance and faith, to Christ who is David's Messiah and ours! See also Galatians 2:16.

    2. Answers will vary. David pictures the Lord as his light when he finds himself in the darkness of uncertainty, as the source of his strength and agility in battle, and as his shield when the enemy attacks. Each picture points to the practical and ever-available help our Lord provides for His people in every age as we find ourselves puzzling over decisions, fending off Satan's animosity and temptations, and facing various troubles, especially persecution for the sake of the Gospel.

    3. Answers will vary; see today's faith narrative.

Thursday—Psalm 18:31–42

    1. Answers will vary.

    2. Answers will vary.

Friday—Psalm 18:43–50

1. The psalm mentions a number of specific things the living God has done for David. For example, the Lord has delivered him from strife and from his enemies; made him head over the nations; given him victory, in some cases, even when he had not "fired a shot" (vv. 44–45); and rescued him from the "man of violence" (v. 48). Other answers are possible.

2. Answers will vary.

Group Bible Study

1. Answers will vary and should be drawn from the text describing the ways the Lord rescued and protected David and the ways He has rescued and protected us in times of danger and turmoil.

2. Listen as group members share. Our God is the God of personal relationship. What good does it do us to know that the Lord rescued Moses, Daniel, and all the rest from danger and defeat if we cannot also rely on Him for help with our own challenges and problems today? In Christ we receive our heavenly Father's personal and individual care. We are not anonymous subscribers to some "group-care policy" with many unknown loopholes! Rather, we are the dearly loved children of the living God, the God who knows us by name, counts each hair on our heads, and has acted to save us in Jesus' death and resurrection.

3. The enemies' attacks on His people have stirred the Lord's anger. He responds most strenuously, racing to rescue His hurting children. Knowing that same fierce love still burns in His heart today, we take great satisfaction and hope, finding confidence and peace in His care for us. Let group members suggest adjectives they find personally meaningful.

4. Answers will vary. Our struggle with these temptations is simply part of the spiritual battle all believers face. Satan knows the power that God has made available to us in His Word. Therefore, the enemy tries to distract us. He magnifies the troubles of life, growling loudly about them and lying to us about the Lord's willingness and ability to help us. We have often "wickedly departed" (v. 21) from our God—cutting ourselves off from the source of our strength. How much we need our Savior! How precious is the sacrifice by which He "purified" us (v. 26) on Calvary's cross!

5. Considering the overwhelming power our Lord possesses, which is so vividly described in Psalm 18, we can readily deduce that we would disappear

in a single puff of smoke were it not that our Jesus is also gentle. Reflect with the members of your group on that gentleness as Isaiah 53 and John 10:11–18 portray it. By His death for our sins, our gentle Savior rescued us from eternal death, making us heirs of heaven. A "wonderful deed," indeed!

6. Answers will vary.

7. Answers will vary.

8. Make a list of the praises and prayer requests as you close; then take turns placing each of these at the throne of grace.

Week 3, Psalm 30

Personal Study Questions

Monday—Psalm 30:1–3

1. Answers will vary.

2. The psalmist exclaims praises to the Lord for several reasons, among them that He has "drawn me up"; "healed me"; "brought up my soul from Sheol"; and "restored me to life." He has "not let my foes rejoice over me."

3. Answers will vary. With David, we focus on our Savior-God, and continue to extol Him, even while the fiery darts continue to rain down upon us. Our Savior-God is our shield; He will not allow Satan to "rejoice over" us (Psalm 30:1). He hears, helps, and heals us (v. 2). In love, He will restore us to life. Although Satan will harass us all our life long, in the end, we will enjoy total peace and full security.

Tuesday—Psalm 30:4–5

1. God's "name" embodies all that He is and all He can do and has done for us. In Scripture, praises to God's name are synonymous with praises to His entire being.

2. The two contrasts are between God's anger (which is momentary) and His favor (which lasts a lifetime) and between weeping (which continues overnight) and joy (which comes in the morning—and stays).

3. Because of our sins, we have deserved God's anger, but just as surely as our Lord has kept His promise to Noah never again to destroy the earth in a cataclysmic flood (Isaiah 54:9), so also He will keep His oath not to be angry with us or rebuke us. Instead, He forgives His repentant people! See the faith

narrative's description of the writer's interaction with her grandpa.

Wednesday—Psalm 30:6–7

1. David stood strong in prosperity, evidently relying as much or more on himself as on the Lord. In concern for the danger in which His child had put himself, the Lord "hid [His] face" and David "was dismayed." Answers to the personal application questions in this question sequence will vary. See today's faith narrative for further insights.

2. Refer back to verse 5 and Isaiah 54:9, on which you meditated yesterday. The Lord teaches and disciplines His children chiefly through His Word (see Psalm 119:33–37). If we refuse to listen and continue down the path of pride toward disaster, negative circumstance may overtake us. However, at many times He may go on blessing us; His "kindness is meant to lead [us] to repentance" (Romans 2:4). All three methods, though, grow out of our Father's heart of love for us and His concern for our eternal well-being.

Thursday—Psalm 30:8–10

1. In this prayer, David pleads for his life and for the mercy that would bring him God's pardon, rather than reinforcing the death penalty his sin rightly deserved. We, too, deserve God's wrath because of our sins of pride and impenitence. We deserve His judgment for the times we have taken His grace for granted, for our unthankful hearts, and for many more sins besides. We "daily sin much and surely deserve nothing but punishment," as the Small Catechism (Fifth Petition) puts it. Without God's mercy, we are lost and "go down to the pit" (v. 9). The psalm is certainly one we could pray daily!

2. Without the Lord's mercy, we find ourselves facing God's judgment and its end, eternal death. As repentant sinners, filled with the joy and relief of God's forgiveness in the cross of our Savior, we can't stop the flow of worship and witness that floods from hearts brim-full of new hope. Worship and witness become for us not a "have-to" but a "get-to."

Friday—Psalm 30:11–12

1. Answers will vary.

2. Answers will vary; in Jesus' perfect life, a life lived in our place and now credited to our account; in His death on the cross for our sins; and in His glorious resurrection victory on Easter, our Savior-God has destroyed death's power, given us victory over sin and Satan, and earned full pardon for every

one of our sins. In doing so, He has brought us many reasons to be thankful. Name some!

3. Answers will vary.

Group Bible Study

1. Answers will vary.

2. Answers will vary. Accept those drawn from the text of the psalm. Then encourage one another to personalize these "wonderful deeds"; when has God acted on your behalf in these ways? Let everyone share as they feel comfortable doing so.

3. Answers will vary. Certainly, we think of the joy we will experience in fullness as we enter heaven's "morning" to live there in glory that knows no end. In addition, we have our Lord's promises in Romans 8:28 and Isaiah 43:2. As God's redeemed, named, baptized heirs, we will go *through* fire and *through* deep waters in this life. But no matter how hot that fire or how threatening that deluge, we belong to Jesus. Nothing will separate us from Him. What examples of this deliverance, these "mornings"—large and small—can participants recall?

4. God made the psalmist's "mountain stand strong," He says, "by [His] favor." Still, David apparently began to rely on outward circumstances, particularly on his material "prosperity," as verse 6 describes it. As Proverbs 2 makes clear, true security lies not in material wealth but in a deep relationship with the Lord, living in the wisdom His Word provides (v. 9) to those who belong to Him through faith. That wisdom is a hidden treasure (Proverbs 2:4), a treasure better than silver. It delivers from death, from evil (vv. 12–13); it involves repentance and faith in the Savior whom God has sent. Still, we often fall back on our material circumstances as we evaluate our security. We are still "people in process"; God has not yet completed our sanctification, His transforming work in our hearts. One day, we will be fully sanctified as we rejoice in heaven's glory forever. For now, we praise Jesus for His cross by which we receive forgiveness for our sins of misbelief, unbelief, and materialism—which is, at its heart, idolatry.

5. After praying for one another, you may want to read Psalm 30 in unison as a fitting summation of your prayer time and an expression of hope in your faithful God.

Week 4, Psalm 31

Personal Study Questions

Monday—Psalm 31:1–5

1. Answers will vary.

2. Answers will vary. In Christ and His cross, our Savior-God has rescued us from sin and its terrible penalties. As verse 5 explains, our God has "redeemed" us, buying us back from Satan and hell—not with silver or gold but with the blood of His own Son.

Tuesday—Psalm 31:6–10

1. Answers will vary.

2. The Lord has seen His affliction, known His distress, delivered Him from the enemy, and set His feet "in a broad place." We certainly have many additional reasons for placing our trust in the Lord; chief among them is God's sacrifice of His only Son on Calvary's cross so we can live with Him in peace, now and forever!

3. Our hearts are prone to mistrust and fear. Remembering God's faithful care for His people in the past and recalling that care as it has been demonstrated to us personally, we can then bring our needs to our Lord with increased boldness and confidence. In Psalm 31, David stumbles into God's presence, as it were, pleading for deliverance and immediate help (vv. 1–7). Then, evidently, the Spirit pulls him up short, taking his focus off the need and placing that focus squarely on God's strength and compassion. (Consider the "for you" in verse 3 and the expressions of trust that follow in verses 4–8.)

4. Answers will vary.

Wednesday—Psalm 31:11–16

1. Some people collect teaspoons or baseball cards; David has (albeit unintentionally) collected enemies! As the object of their plots and destructive schemes, David finds himself isolated, bystanders unwilling to associate with him, perhaps fearing they may wind up on the list of collateral damage. Sad to say, God's people still endure this kind of loneliness. Office politics, family quarrels, and even infighting among people in the church can lead to polarization, isolation, and the pain these cause.

2. The "You" in verse 14 contrasts with the acquaintances, neighbors, and friends who have deserted David. Sinners all, human beings will let us down—sometimes intentionally when it's in their best interests to abandon us, sometimes unintentionally due to their personal limitations and the magnitude of our need. Even presidents and princes grow old, get sick, and die. Only our Lord is fully and eternally trustworthy! He will always be our God; He holds us in His hands. He has made each day and each moment of our lives His concern. The hands that hold us safe still bear the scars of the wounds by which He won our salvation.

3. Answers will vary.

Thursday—Psalm 31:17–20

1. Answers will vary.

2. Answers will vary.

3. Answers will vary but may include friends experiencing difficulty with strife and, in particular, other believers around the world who face persecution, pain, imprisonment, and even death because of their love for Jesus.

Friday—Psalm 31:21–24

1. The psalmist feels alarm and experiences the sensation of being cut off from the Lord, abandoned by Him. In reality, the Lord has heard his every plea. God's determined, persistent love has not changed, despite the emotions the psalmist feels.

2. Answers will vary. See today's faith narrative for further insights.

Group Bible Study

1. Answers will vary; accept those drawn from the text that align with the accounts given to us through the evangelists—Matthew, Mark, Luke, and John. Participants will likely diverge from one another as they suggest situations in which they may turn to Psalm 31 for comfort and support. Accept reasonable responses.

2. Answers will vary.

3. Answers will vary; many psalms follow this same approach or pattern.

4. Answers will vary. Probably most of us pray most of the time the way David does in Psalm 31. We are each a bundle of needs! We can come

into God's presence secure in the fact that we will be heard, despite our lack of preparation and regardless of how logically our thoughts and words flow forth. Prayer is like having a conversation, not giving a speech or presentation. We share our feelings and burdens with our friend Jesus, knowing He accepts us for the sake of His cross.

Let participants cite examples of the psalmist's respectful attitude. While past generations may have overdone the formality of prayer, praying mostly as they read prayers written by someone else, we in our time probably overdo the informality, talking with our Lord as though He were one of our bowling buddies! We need constantly to keep in mind our creatureliness and His glorious holiness, His "otherness." We enter His presence only at His invitation and by His grace, only by the blood of the Lamb!

5. Answers will vary. Base today's closing prayer on needs that surface during this discussion.

Week 5, Psalm 32

Personal Study Questions

Monday—Psalm 32:1–4

1. Answers will vary. Synonyms for *forgiveness* include "covered" and "not counted." Other responses are possible, depending on the Bible version one is using.

2. At first, facing his sin, David "kept silent." We may deceive ourselves about our sin by refusing to examine our own hearts, by trying to go on as if nothing has happened, or by downplaying the seriousness of our offenses against God. Or we may fool ourselves into thinking we can somehow make up for our guilt by doing some kind of community service in our family, our church, or at work. In reality, none of this deceives or satisfies an angry God. Instead, He invites us to confess and receive the forgiveness Jesus won for us in His cross. Scripture repeats and repeats His assurances of pardon, His promises of hope. See today's faith narrative for more insights.

Tuesday—Psalm 32:5

1. Answers will vary; verses 3–4 contain several descriptions of the agony David experienced before he finally confessed. But when he did, God forgave completely. Examples of similar, personal experiences will vary.

2. Our feeling terrible for any number of days does nothing to reduce the guilt we bear on account of our sin. It in no way makes up for our guilt. Jesus bore our punishment in full. Far better when facing a guilty conscience to acknowledge our sin at once, to receive God's full forgiveness through faith in His Son, and then perhaps to spend our energy doing all we can to repair the damage we have caused—working to restore a wounded relationship, finding ways to make financial restitution, correcting the misimpression we have left by our gossip, or in some other way demonstrating heartfelt repentance. The practice of private Confession and Absolution is always a spiritually healthy practice; those who struggle often with a guilty conscience may find it especially helpful.

3. Answers will vary. See today's faith narrative.

Wednesday—Psalm 32:6–7

1. David is saying to us, in essence, "God forgives, so go ahead and pray, confessing your sin. Don't wait in misery like I did. No matter how deep (or how hot!) the water in which you find yourself, you have a hiding place. Run to Him!" We hide in the wounds of our crucified and risen Lord Jesus and need not, thus, hesitate to come to Him immediately in every need, especially when our need is for forgiveness. See today's faith narrative for additional insights.

2. Answers will vary, but what better truth to meditate upon than the Lord as our hiding place from guilt, sin, and iniquity!

3. God rejoices in our repentance, but so do the holy angels and, often, other believers right here on earth. How comforting and encouraging! We can add this joy to the list of many reasons for being quick to repent, quick to confess.

Thursday—Psalm 32:8–9

1. Answers will vary. David seems to be saying that even as a practical matter, from a purely human perspective, it's better to repent and be forgiven than to rebel and endure the consequences. David had tried to figure out his dilemma on his own, ignoring God's Law and paying a terrible price as a re-

sult. Now, he encourages us to have the humility to obey the Lord's direction immediately!

2. Answers will vary.

3. Answers will vary.

Friday—Psalm 32:10–11

1. Because we "daily sin much," all human beings—believers and unbelievers alike—are "wicked."

2. The best answer to this question is simply, "I am righteous because Jesus died for me." This is what theologians call "imputed righteousness" and comes to us as a gift from God because of what He did for us in Jesus. Now, "steadfast love surrounds the one who trusts in the LORD" (v. 10).

3. Answers will vary. If we had to live without the confidence that our sins were completely forgiven, even the most wonderful life on earth would be miserable as we awaited the terrible consequences of everlasting death in hell's dreadful prison. Additionally, Christians count an ongoing relationship of love for and trust in Jesus here on earth as our highest treasure. No toys or trinkets the earth offers could replace it!

Group Bible Study

1. Answers will vary. The pardon we receive in Jesus and in His cross is the premier gift God gives, the crown jewel among all the many "wonderful deeds" for which we praise Him. Without this gift, we could not truly and eternally enjoy any other blessing of our Lord.

2. Answers will vary.

3. Invite participants to speculate about reasons behind the continuing "culture of cover up" among leaders in government and business. Then ask for comments closer to home; why do we tend to cover up instead of 'fessing up? Our reasons for avoiding honest confession probably boil down to one of three concerns: fear, shame, or pain avoidance. Avoiding confession results in misery, continuing confusion, and ineffectiveness in our witness to our Lord; repentance and faith opens the door for Jesus' pardon, healing, and hope.

4. All the other penitential psalms begin with words of confession or a description of the wretched conditions sin has worked in the psalmist's life. Psalm 32 begins on a note of joy and goes on to describe the blessed state

resulting from sins forgiven. Psalm 32 describes the blessings and benefits of confession; the other psalms listed are actual prayers of confession offered by the psalmist when caught up in a state of guilt. In this sense, Psalm 32 is more instructional, while the other penitential psalms are more liturgical or devotional. These distinctions may help point participants to further uses of all six penitential psalms.

    5. Answers will vary.

Week 6, Psalm 106

Personal Study Questions

Monday—Psalm 106:1–12

    1. Answers will vary. Verses 1–12 include several examples.

    2. Answers will vary. The faith narrative includes several examples.

    3. Answers will vary.

Tuesday—Psalm 106:13–23

    1. Answers will vary but should include the idea that idols include anyone or anything on which we rely for life's ultimate good, for our life's true meaning and purpose, or as our only true source of help in times of trouble.

    2. Answers will vary.

    3. At Calvary, Jesus not only pleaded for mercy on our behalf, He also took the punishment we had by our sins deserved. Now as our eternal High Priest, He continues to pray for us, as the text from Hebrews 10 makes clear.

Wednesday—Psalm 106:24–33

    1. Answers will vary.

    2. Answers will vary.

Thursday—Psalm 106:34–43

    1. Answers will vary; today's faith narrative gives several specific, pertinent examples.

    2. Answers will vary.

    3. Answers will vary. See today's faith narrative.

Friday—Psalm 106:44–48

1. Answers will vary.

2. See Matthew 25:3–40. Ultimately, God's people will find rescue, peace, and joy after He "gather[s] us from the nations" (Psalm 106:47) on the Last Day and as we celebrate His mercy and grace in His eternal presence in the glories of heaven. Even now, though, we enjoy a "foretaste of the feast to come" as we worship together, share informally around God's Word in Bible study, and participate in the Lord's Supper with Christ and one another.

Group Bible Study

1. Answers will vary.

2. Answers will vary, depending upon which historical events and details each partner pair chooses as a focus. Share insights with one another as time will allow. Someone should note the time so your group spends no more than fifteen to twenty minutes on this set of questions.

3. Psalm 106 stands as a stern warning against repeating the pattern of sin God's people have enacted in the past. It also provides ample reassurance that "the steadfast love of the Lord never ceases; His mercies never come to an end" (Lamentations 3:22; see also Malachi 3:16). As you talk about today's culture, avoid judgmentally confessing the sins of others, even as you help one another see the dangers embedded in adopting practices that easily lead to rebellion and apostasy.

4. Despite our rebellion, Jesus continually prays for us before the Father's throne; God hears our Savior's prayers for mercy, based on the death of His Son and the blood Christ shed for us on Calvary's cross. Talk together about the blessings of being able to intercede for others. In the verse from James' epistle, God promises to hear the prayers His people pray for one another; we can trust His promises!

5. Accept answers drawn from the text. Answers may vary somewhat depending upon which Bible translation(s) participants have been using.

For the complete A New Song experience try the Small-Group DVD Kit!

Each Small-Group DVD Kit Includes:
- 1 DVD
- 5 copies of the Bible study
- Promotional materials

A New Song titles available:

Planted by Streams of Water

Small-Group DVD Kit
20-3434EGA

Bible Study Book
20-3404EGA

I Have Set My King on Zion

Small-Group DVD Kit
20-3435EGA

Bible Study Book
20-3405EGA

Save Me, O My God!

Small-Group DVD Kit
20-3444EGA

Bible Study Book
20-3440EGA

All of Your Wonderful Deeds

Small-Group DVD Kit
20-3445EGA

Bible Study Book
20-3441EGA

To order call 1-800-325-3040 or visit cph.org